365 Stories and Rhymes for Girls

Every effort has been made to acknowledge the contributors to this book.
If we have made any errors, we will be pleased to rectify them in future editions.

This edition published by Parragon in 2007

Parragon
Queen Street House
4 Queen Street
Bath BA1 1HE, UK

Design and project management by Aztec Design

Page make-up by
Mik Martin, Caroline Reeves, and Kilnwood Graphics

ISBN 978-1-4054-7872-4
Printed in China

365 Stories and Rhymes for Girls

Bath · New York · Singapore · Hong Kong · Cologne · Delhi · Melbourne

Contents

The Little Doll

I once had a sweet little doll, dears,
  The prettiest doll in the world;
Her cheeks were so red and so white, dears,
  And her hair was so charmingly curled.
But I lost my poor little doll, dears,
  As I played in the heath one day;
And I cried for her more than a week, dears;
  But I never could find where she lay.

I found my poor little doll, dears,
  As I played in the heath one day:
Folks say she is terribly changed, dears,
  For her paint is all washed away,
And her arm trodden off
  by the cows, dears,
And her hair not the least
  bit curled:
    Yet for old sakes' sake
    she is still, dears,
    The prettiest doll
    in the world.

There was an Old Man from Peru

There was an old man from Peru
  Who dreamed he was eating his shoe.
He woke in a fright
  In the middle of the night
And found it was perfectly true.

Minnie and Winnie

Minnie and Winnie
  Slept in a shell.
Sleep, little ladies!
  And they slept well.

Pink was the shell within,
  Silver without;
Sounds of the great sea
  Wandered about.

Sleep, little ladies,
  Wake not soon!
Echo on echo
  Dies to the moon.

Two bright stars
  Peeped into the shell.
"What are they dreaming of?
  Who can tell?"

Started a green linnet
  Out of the croft;
Wake, little ladies,
  The sun is aloft!

ALFRED, LORD TENNYSON

Brother and Sister

"Sister, sister go to bed!
    Go and rest your weary head."
Thus the prudent brother said.

"Do you want a battered hide,
    Or scratches to your face applied?"
Thus his sister calm replied.

"Sister, do not raise my wrath.
    I'd make you into mutton broth
As easily as kill a moth!"

The sister raised her beaming eye
    And looked on him indignantly
And sternly answered, "Only try!"

Off to the cook he quickly ran.
    "Dear Cook, please lend a frying-pan
To me as quickly as you can."

"And wherefore should I lend it you?"
    "The reason, Cook, is plain to view.
I wish to make an Irish stew."

"What meat is in that stew to go?"
    "My sister'll be the contents!"
        "Oh!"
"You'll lend the pan to me, Cook?"
"No!"

Moral: Never stew your sister.
LEWIS CARROLL

Skipping

Little children skip,
    The rope so gaily gripping,
Tom and Harry,
    Jane and Mary,
Kate, Diana,
    Susan, Anna,
All are fond of skipping!

The little boats they skip,
    Beside the heavy shipping,
And while the squalling
    Winds are calling,
Falling, rising,
    Rising, falling,
All are fond
    of skipping!

I Eat my Peas with Honey

I eat my peas with honey,
    I've done it all my life,
It makes the peas taste funny,
    But it keeps them on my knife.

11

Cinderella

Once upon a time, there lived a very pretty girl. Sadly, when she was young, her mother died. Her father remarried, but the girl's stepmother was a mean woman with two ugly daughters. These stepsisters were so jealous of the young girl's beauty that they treated her like a servant and made her sit among the cinders in the kitchen.

They called her Cinderella, and before long everyone, even her father, had forgotten the poor girl's real name. Cinderella missed her real mother more and more each day.

One day, an invitation arrived from the royal palace. The king and queen were holding a ball for the prince's twenty-first birthday, and all the fine ladies of the kingdom were invited.

Cinderella's stepsisters were very excited when their invitations to the ball arrived.

"I will wear my red velvet gown!" cried the first stepsister. "And the black pearl necklace that Mother gave to me."

"And I will wear my blue silk dress with a silver tiara!" cried the other.

"Come, Cinderella!" they called. "You must help us to get ready!"

Cinderella helped her stepsisters with their silk stockings and frilly petticoats. She brushed and curled their hair and powdered their cheeks and noses. At last, she squeezed them into their beautiful ball gowns.

But, even after all this, the two ugly stepsisters weren't nearly as lovely as Cinderella was in her rags. This made them very jealous and angry, and they began to tease Cinderella.

"Too bad you can't come to the ball, Cinders!" sneered the first stepsister.

"Yes," laughed the other one. "They'd never let a shabby creature like you near the palace!"

Cinderella said nothing, but inside, her heart was breaking. She really wanted to go to the ball. After her stepsisters left, she sat and wept.

"Dry your tears, my dear," said a gentle voice.

Cinderella was amazed. A kind old woman stood before her. In her hand was a sparkly wand that shone.

"I am your fairy godmother," she told Cinderella. "And you shall go to the ball!"

"But I have nothing to wear! How will I get there?" cried Cinderella.

The fairy godmother smiled.

The fairy godmother asked Cinders to fetch her the biggest pumpkin in the garden. With a flick of her magic wand she turned it into a golden carriage and the mice in the kitchen mousetrap into fine horses. A fat rat soon became a handsome coachman.

Cinderella could not believe her eyes.

Smiling, the fairy godmother waved her wand once more and suddenly Cinderella was dressed in a splendid ball gown. On her feet were sparkling glass slippers.

"My magic will end at midnight, so you must be home before then," said the fairy godmother. "Good luck."

When Cinderella arrived at the ball, everyone was dazzled by her beauty. Whispers went round the ballroom as the other guests wondered who this enchanting stranger could be. Even Cinderella's own stepsisters did not recognise her.

As soon as the prince set eyes on Cinderella, he fell in love with her. "Would you do me the honour of this dance?" he asked.

"Why certainly, sir," Cinderella answered.
And from that moment on he only had eyes for Cinderella.

Soon the clock struck midnight. "I must go!" said Cinderella, suddenly remembering her promise to her fairy godmother. She fled from the ballroom and ran down the palace steps. The prince ran after her, but when he got outside, she was gone. He didn't notice a grubby servant girl holding a pumpkin. A few mice and a rat scurried around her feet.

But there on the steps was one dainty glass slipper. The prince picked it up and rushed back into the palace. "Does anyone know who this slipper belongs to?" he cried.

The next day, Cinderella's stepsisters could talk of nothing but the ball, and the beautiful stranger who had danced all night with the prince. As they were talking, there was a knock at the door.

"Cinderella," called the stepmother, "quick, jump to it and see who it is." Standing on the doorstep was His Highness the Prince and a royal footman, who was holding the little glass slipper on a velvet cushion.

"The lady whose foot this slipper fits is my one and only true love," said the prince. "I am visiting every house in the kingdom in search of her."

The two stepsisters began shoving each other out of the way in their rush to try on the slipper. They both squeezed and pushed as hard as they could, but their clumsy feet were far too big for the tiny glass shoe.

Then Cinderella stepped forward. "Please, Your Highness," she said, shyly, "may I try?"

As her stepsisters watched in utter amazement, Cinderella slid her foot into the dainty slipper. It fitted as if it were made for her!

As the prince gazed into her eyes, he knew he had found his love – and Cinderella knew she had found hers.

Cinderella and the prince soon set a date to be married.

On the day of their wedding, the land rang to the sound of bells, and the sun shone as the people cheered. Even Cinderella's nasty stepsisters were invited. Everyone had a really wonderful day, and Cinderella and her prince lived happily ever after.

Cock Crow

The cock's on the wood pile
  Blowing his horn,
The bull's in the barn
  A-threshing the corn,
The maids in the meadow
  Are making the hay,
The ducks in the river
  Are swimming away.

The Old Woman's Three Cows

There was an old woman had three cows,
  Rosy and Colin and Dun.
Rosy and Colin were sold at the fair,
  And Dun broke her heart in a fit of despair,
So there was an end of her three cows,
  Rosy and Colin and Dun.

An Apple a Day

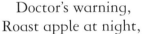

An apple a day
  Sends the doctor away.
Apple in the morning
  Doctor's warning,
Roast apple at night,
  Starves the doctor outright.
Eat an apple going to bed,
  Knock the doctor on the head.
Three each day, seven days a week.
  Ruddy apple, ruddy cheek.

Sing, Sing

Sing, sing,
  What shall I sing?
The cat's run away
  With the pudding string!
Do, do,
  What shall I do?
The cat's run away
  With the pudding too!

To the Snail

Snail, snail, put out
  your horns,
And I will give you bread
  and barley corns.

Sulky Sue

Here's Sulky Sue
  What shall we do?
Turn her face to the wall
  'Til she comes to.

Little Poll Parrot

Little Poll Parrot
   Sat in his garret
Eating toast and tea;
   A little brown mouse
Jumped into the house,
   And stole it all away.

I Had a Little Horse

I had a little horse,
   His name was Dappled Grey,
His head was made of gingerbread,
   His tail was made of hay.
He could amble, he could trot,
   He could carry the mustard pot,
He could amble, he could trot,
   Through the old town of Windsor.

The Legacy

My father died a month ago
   And left me all his riches;
A feather bed, a wooden leg,
   And a pair of leather breeches;
A coffee pot without a spout,
   And a cup without a handle,
A tobacco pipe without a lid,
   And half a farthing candle.

One for the Mouse

One for the Mouse
   One for the house,
One for the crow,
   One to rot,
One to grow.

Roses are Red

Roses are red,
   Violets are blue,
Sugar is sweet
   And so are you.

Ballerina Belle

Belle the ballerina is a beautiful ballet dancer. She loves to dance in her frilly tutu and satin ballet shoes. She has a best friend – Pearl, a fluffy white kitten with big blue eyes. Pearl enjoys watching Belle dance, spinning and twirling across the floor.

Today Belle is getting ready for a very special show. The little kitten sits on her friend's pink dressing table purring with delight, as Belle carefully dusts a sprinkling of powder over her face.

Belle is so excited and nervous. Tonight, she will dance for the King and Queen.

Pearl purrs her approval as the little ballerina puts on a blue tutu that glistens with jewels. Then she ties the pretty ribbons on her shoes. Finally, Belle puts up her lovely long hair with silver hairpins. Pearl thinks she looks wonderful. Now Belle is all ready for the show and tiptoes to the stage...

The music starts and Belle begins to twirl gracefully across the floor. The King and Queen love to watch her dance – she is the most beautiful ballerina ever.

As the audience cheers, Pearl purrs with delight. Belle's the happiest ballerina in the world.

Lucy and the Green Door

Lucy Jenkins lived in an ordinary house, in an ordinary street, in an ordinary town. At the back of Lucy's house was an ordinary garden with ordinary flowers and an ordinary path. But down the path at the bottom of the garden was a tree that was not ordinary at all! It was a huge old oak tree, and at the bottom of the tree was a very small green door, only just big enough for Lucy to squeeze through. This was Lucy's secret, because only she knew about the door. But what lay behind the door was Lucy's best secret of all!

Each afternoon Lucy would knock lightly on the door. On the third knock the door would swing open wide, and the chief elf would be there to welcome her inside.

"Come in for tea, little Lucy," the elf would always say.

Inside, Lucy would meet some very special friends indeed! First there were Penelope and Geraldine, two of the gentlest and sweetest fairies it was possible to imagine.

Then there were Basil and Granville, who were rather mischievous imps. And there were the storytellers, who would sit for hours with Lucy and tell her the greatest tales from all the corners of the world. And of course there was the chief elf, who would make the most delicious milkshakes and scones with heaps of cream for Lucy to eat.

The world behind the green door was a wonderful place, and Lucy would always go home afterwards feeling very cheerful and jolly. On one particular visit to the world behind the green door Lucy had just finished a scrumptious tea of cocoa and toasted marshmallows with the chief elf, when she went off to play games with Basil and Granville.

Now just recently, Lucy had been feeling down in the dumps because very soon she would be going to school and would only be able to visit her friends at weekends. But they assured her that they would never forget her, and that as long as she was always a true friend to them she could visit as often or as little as she liked. This cheered up Lucy considerably, and then they took her to visit the storytellers so that her happiness was complete. Of all the delights behind the green door, the storytellers were Lucy's favourite. They told her stories of how the whales had learned to sing, and of where the stars went when the sun had risen in the sky and they had slipped from view.

Because of the assurances of the fairies, Lucy was not too worried when the day came for her to start school. Lucy would go to school each day and then afterwards would visit her friends behind the green door. As winter came round and the days grew dark she only visited at weekends, and looked forward to the holidays when she could visit them every day again.

Meanwhile, at school, Lucy had made friends with a girl called Jessica, and, although she told Jessica all about her family and her home, she didn't at first tell her about her special tree with the little green door and its magic world. But Lucy did tell Jessica the stories that she was told by the storytellers, and Jessica grew very curious about where she had heard all the wonderful tales. Every day, Jessica would ask more questions, and Lucy found it harder to avoid telling her about her secret. Eventually, Lucy gave in and told Jessica all about her adventures behind the green door.

Jessica scoffed and laughed. She howled with laughter at the thought of the wonderful teas and the stories that followed. Jessica thought that Lucy was making the whole thing up! When Lucy protested, Jessica told her that it simply wasn't possible – that there were no such things as elves and fairies and imps and strange and wonderful worlds behind doors in trees. So Lucy decided to show Jessica.

On the way home Lucy started to worry. What if she really had imagined it all? But, if her wonderful friends didn't exist, how could she possibly know them? Jessica walked beside Lucy, still teasing her and laughing about Lucy's "invisible" friends!

Lucy and Jessica reached the bottom of the garden. Just as Lucy was about to tap lightly on the green door she suddenly noticed the door had disappeared. She rubbed her eyes and looked again, but it had gone!

Jessica laughed at Lucy, calling her silly and babyish to believe in magic and fairy tales, and then ran off back to school.

Lucy could not face going back to school that afternoon, and when her mother saw her she thought she must be ill – she looked so upset! Lucy went up to bed and she cried herself to sleep.

And when Lucy slept she started to dream. All the imps, elves, fairies and the storytellers were there in the dream. Then they hugged her and asked why she hadn't been to see them for so long. Lucy explained what had happened on her last visit, and then Geraldine spoke. "Little Lucy," she said, "you are special. You believe in magic and you believe in the little people. And, because you believe, you are able to see us and live among us. But those who don't believe will always be shut out from our world. You must keep your belief, little Lucy."

With a huge surge of happiness Lucy woke up, dressed quickly and ran out of her ordinary house, down the ordinary path in the ordinary garden up to the extraordinary tree, and was delighted to see the green door once more! She knocked very lightly and, after the third tap, the door swung open to reveal the chief elf. "Come inside, little Lucy," the elf said happily, "and have some tea."

One Snowy Day

One snowy day, Old Bear poked his nose out of his den, and saw the deep snow that had fallen while he slept. "I'll take a stroll in the woods," he said. Off he went, his great paws padding along, as big white snowflakes tickled his nose. How he loved the snow! He walked far into the woods, deep in thought, and quite forgot to look where he was going.

After a while, Old Bear stopped and looked around. To his dismay, he realised he was quite lost. Then he spied the trail of pawprints behind him. "Ho, ho!" he chuckled. "I'm not lost at all! I can follow my pawprints home!" And, thinking what a clever old bear he was, he carried on walking, until at last he began to feel tired. "I'll just take a rest," he said to himself. He closed his eyes, and soon fell fast asleep. Meanwhile, the snow kept on falling...

By the time Old Bear woke up his trail of pawprints had disappeared! "Now I'll never find my way home!" he groaned. Then, he noticed an old tree stump nearby.

"That looks familiar. And so does that fallen log over there. If I'm not mistaken, I've walked in a big circle, and ended up at home!" he chuckled, turning towards his den. "What a clever old bear I am, after all!"

The Walrus and the Carpenter

"The time has come," the Walrus said,
  "To talk of many things:
Of shoes – and ships – and sealing-wax –
  Of cabbages – and kings –
And why the sea is boiling hot –
  And whether pigs have wings."

"But wait a bit," the Oysters cried,
  "Before we have our chat;
For some of us are out of breath,
  And all of us are fat!"
"No hurry!" said the carpenter.
  They thanked him much for that.

"A load of bread," the Walrus said,
  "Is what we chiefly need:
Pepper and vinegar besides
  Are very good indeed –
Now if you're ready, Oysters dear,
  We can begin to feed."

Lady Moon

Lady Moon, Lady Moon,
  Where are you roving?
  Over the sea.
Lady Moon, Lady Moon,
  Whom are you loving?
  All that love me.
Are you not tired with
  Rolling, and never
  Resting to sleep?
Why look so pale,
  And so sad, as for ever
  Wishing to weep?

Ariel's Song

Full fathom five thy father lies;
  Of his bones are coral made;
Those are pearls that were his eyes:
  Nothing of him that doth fade,
But doth suffer a sea-change
  Into something rich and strange:
Sea nymphs hourly ring his knell.
  Ding-dong!
Hark! now I hear them,
  Ding-dong, bell!

There's a Hole in the Middle of the Sea

There's a hole, there's a hole,
  there's a hole in the middle of the sea.
There's a log in the hole in the middle
  of the sea.
There's a hole, there's a hole,
  there's a hole in the middle of the sea.
There's a bump on the log in the
  hole in the middle of the sea.
There's a hole, there's a hole,
  there's a hole in the middle
  of the sea.

There's a frog on the bump on the
  log in the hole in the middle of
  the sea.
There's a hole, there's a hole, there's
  a hole in the middle of the sea.
There's a fly on the frog on the bump
  on the log in the hole in the middle
  of the sea.
There's a hole, there's a hole, there's
  a hole in the middle of the sea.

Small is the Wren

Small is the wren,
  Black is the rook,
Great is the sinner
  That steals this book.

The Children's Hour

Between the dark and the daylight,
  When the night is beginning to lower,
Comes a pause in the day's occupations,
  That is known as the Children's Hour.

I hear in the chamber above me
  The patter of little feet,
The sound of a door that is opened,
  And voices soft and sweet.

From my study I see in the lamplight,
  Descending the broad hall stair,
Grave Alice, and laughing Allegra,
  And Edith with golden hair.

A whisper, and then a silence:
  Yet I know by their
    merry eyes
They are plotting and
    planning together
To take me by surprise.

Poorly Bear

Teddy Bear came home from school feeling tired and poorly. "I don't want my hot chocolate," he told Mummy Bear. Teddy Bear sat on the sofa and closed his eyes. "And I don't want to watch television either," he said.

"Do you want to play your drum?" asked Mummy Bear, looking worried. Teddy Bear shook his head, so Mummy Bear went to fetch the thermometer and she put it under Teddy Bear's tongue. "Oh dear," she said. "I'm afraid you're a very poorly Teddy Bear. Up to bed you go!"

The next morning Teddy Bear was covered all over in bright red spots. "Look at me!" he said proudly, showing off his belly.

"You've got chicken pox," said Mummy Bear. "You'll have to stay home from school today."

"Yippee!" said Teddy Bear. But he said it quietly, because his head was quite sore. Teddy Bear lay on the sofa all day, watching television and colouring some pictures. Mummy Bear read him stories and brought him soup and ice cream to eat.

After a few days the spots disappeared.

"Can I play my drum?" asked Teddy Bear. Mummy Bear was so glad to see Teddy Bear looking well again, that she let him play his drum for the rest of the afternoon.

Hungry Bear

"I'm hungry!" said Teddy Bear.

"You've just finished your lunch," said Mummy Bear. "You can have something in a little while."

"But I want something now!" wailed Teddy Bear. "I'm starving!"

"If you eat any more you'll go pop!" said Mummy Bear.

"I only want a biscuit! Or ice cream. Or maybe a piece of cake. I'm really hungry!" grumbled Teddy Bear. He went outside and made hungry faces through the window.

"You don't look hungry," said Betty Bear from next door.

"I am!" said Teddy Bear. Nobody else came by, so Teddy Bear climbed into his sandpit. He dug some roads and built a few houses. He built a huge castle on a hill, with a moat around it. Then he fetched some water from the garden tap and filled the moat.

"Teddy!" called Mummy Bear. "You can come inside now and have some cakes!"

But Teddy Bear just shook his head – he was having far too much fun to feel hungry any more!

The Princess and the Pea

Once upon a time, there was a prince whose dearest wish was to marry a princess – but only a true princess would do. In order to find her, he travelled far and wide, all over the land.

He met young princesses and old ones, beautiful princesses and plain ones, rich princesses and poor ones, but there was always something that was not quite right with each of them.

The prince began to despair. He called together his courtiers and announced, "I have failed to find my dream princess. We will go home to our palace without delay."

One dark night, back at his palace; there was the most tremendous storm. Lightning flashed across the sky and thunder buffeted the thick palace walls.

The prince and his parents were talking in the drawing room. He was telling them all about his hopeless search for a perfect princess to marry. "Don't despair, dear," said his mother, the queen. "Who knows what surprises the future may hold. You could find your perfect princess when you least expect to."

Just then, they heard a tiny tap-tapping at the window. The prince opened it, and standing there before him was a very beautiful, but very wet, young lady. Her hair was dripping, her dress was soaked through, and she was shivering with cold.

"I am a princess," she told the prince, "and I am lost. Please may I come in and shelter from the storm?"

The prince was astonished. He asked the girl into the palace, then he turned to the queen and whispered in her ear, "Oh, Mother, she is enchanting! But how can I be sure she really is a princess?"

"Leave it to me," said his mother, and she hurried off to have a bedroom prepared for the pretty girl.

First, the queen placed a little green pea on the mattress. Then she ordered the servants to bring twenty thick mattresses, and twenty feather quilts, which they piled on top of the pea. The princess needed a very tall ladder to climb into bed that night!

The next morning, at breakfast, the queen asked the princess if she had slept well.

"I had the most awful night!" said the princess. "I don't know what it was, but there was a hard lump under my bed, and it kept me awake all night, and now I'm absolutely covered with bruises!"

"At last!" the queen exclaimed, "our search is over! We have found a true princess for our son. Only a real princess would have

skin so tender that she could feel a pea through twenty mattresses and twenty feather quilts!"

The prince was overjoyed, and he and the princess were soon married.

As for the little green pea, the prince had a special cabinet made and it was put on display in the royal museum, where it can still be seen today!

There was a Naughty Boy

There was a naughty boy,
A naughty boy was he,
He would not stop at home,
He could not quiet be –
He took
In his knapsack
A book
Full of vowels
And a shirt
With some towels,
A slight cap
For nightcap,
A hair brush,
Comb ditto,
New stockings –
For old ones
Would split O!
This knapsack
Tight at's back
He rivetted close
And followed his nose
To the North,
To the North,
And followed his nose
To the North.

JOHN KEATS

Where are you Going to, My Pretty Maid?

Where are you going to, my pretty maid?
    Where are you going to, my pretty maid?
I'm going a-milking, sir, she said,
    Sir, she said, sir, she said,
I'm going a-milking, sir, she said.

May I go with you, my pretty maid?
    May I go with you, my pretty maid?
You're kindly welcome, sir, she said,
    Sir, she said, sir, she said,
You're kindly welcome, sir, she said.

What is your fortune, my pretty maid?
    What is your fortune, my pretty maid?
My face is my fortune, sir, she said,
    Sir, she said, sir, she said,
My face is my fortune, sir, she said.

Then I can't marry you, my pretty maid,
    Then I can't marry you, my pretty maid,
        Nobody asked you, sir, she said,
        Sir, she said, sir, she said,
            Nobody asked you, sir, she said.

A Frog he Would a-Wooing Go

A frog he would a-wooing go,
  Heigho! says Rowley,
Whether his mother would let him or no,
  With a rowley, powley, gammon and spinach.

A Candle

Little Nancy Etticoat
  In a white petticoat,
And a red rose.
  The longer she stands
The shorter she grows.

A Tisket, a Tasket

A tisket, a tasket,
  A green and yellow basket.
I wrote a letter to my love,
  And on the way I dropped it.

I dropped it, I dropped it,
  And on the way I dropped it.
A little girl picked it up
  And put it in her pocket.

The City Child

Dainty little maiden, whither would you wander?
  Whither from this pretty home, the home where mother dwells?
"Far and far away," said the dainty little maiden,
  "All among the gardens, auriculas, anemones,
Roses and lilies and Canterbury-bells."

Dainty little maiden, whither would you wander?
  Whither from this pretty house, this city house of ours?
"Far and far away," said the dainty little maiden,
  "All among the meadows, the clover and the clematis,
Daisies and kingcups and honeysuckle-flowers."

ALFRED, LORD TENNYSON

The Toys that Ran Away

"Put your toys away, Lucy," said Lucy's mother, "it's time for bed." Lucy gave a great big sigh. "Do I really have to?" she asked, knowing full well what the answer was going to be.

"Of course you do," said her mother. "You shouldn't have to be told to put your toys away. You really don't look after them properly."

It was true. Lucy never had been very good at looking after her toys. Once she left her beautiful new doll outside in her pram and she had become ruined after it rained. Then she had carelessly dropped her tea set on the floor and some of the cups had broken. And she was forever just pushing all her toys back in the cupboard in a hurry, instead of putting them away carefully. Worse still, when she was in a temper, she would throw her toys, and sometimes she would even kick them.

Tonight Lucy was in another of her "can't be bothered" moods. She grabbed some dolls and a teddy and threw them into the cupboard. Without even looking behind her, Lucy picked up some puzzles and a skipping rope, and tossed them into the cupboard, too. They landed with a crash on top of the other toys. Then Lucy closed the cupboard door, squashing the toys even more, and went to have her bath.

Inside the toy cupboard Teddy said, "I'm not going to stay here a moment longer. I'm leaving for good."

"So am I!" said Katie, the ragdoll.

"I want to be somewhere where I'm not thrown around," said one of the puzzles.

One after another the toys decided they would all go back to Toyland and wait to be given to some children who would love them more.

The next morning, Lucy decided to play with some toys but, when she opened the toy cupboard, she couldn't believe her eyes!

All the toys had vanished. The shelves were completely empty. All day, Lucy searched high and low for her missing

toys, but they were nowhere to be found. She went to bed in tears, and wondered if she would ever be able to play with her toys again.

That night, Lucy was suddenly woken by a noise in her bedroom. Was she seeing things or was that a little fairy at the bottom of her bed? "Who are you?" asked Lucy.

"I am the special messenger from Toyland," replied the fairy. "I have been sent to tell you that all your toys have run away back to Toyland, because you treated them badly."

"Oh, I do miss my toys so much," cried Lucy.

With that, the fairy floated over to Lucy, took her hand and lifted Lucy off her bed. They both flew out of Lucy's bedroom window, across fields and forests, until it became too misty to see anything at all. Then they floated down to the ground and the mist lifted, and Lucy found herself in the grounds of a huge fairy-tale castle.

"This is Toyland Castle," explained the fairy. Lucy found herself in a large, cosy room with a huge log fire. Sitting in the corner was a kindly looking little man wearing a carpenter's apron and holding a broken wooden doll. "Hello," he said, "you've come to ask your toys to return, haven't you?"

"Well… er… yes," said Lucy, not really knowing what to say.

"It's up to them to decide, of course," said the little man. "They only come back here if they are mistreated. If they are broken, I repair them, and then they go to other children who love them more."

"But I do love my toys," wept Lucy.

"Then come and tell them yourself," smiled the little man, and he led Lucy into another room. There, to her surprise, were all her toys. Not only that, but they were all shiny and new again. Nothing was broken or chipped or scratched.

Lucy ran up to her toys. "Please, toys, please come home again. I really do love you and miss you, and I promise I shall never mistreat you again," she cried, and then she hugged all the toys.

"Well, it's up to the toys now," said the little man. "You must go back home again with the fairy messenger and hope that they will give you another chance."

With that, the fairy messenger took Lucy's hand. Soon they were floating over her own garden and through her bedroom window. Lucy was so tired she fell asleep as soon as she got into bed.

In the morning she awoke, still rather sleepy, and rushed to the toy cupboard. There, neatly lined up on the shelves, were all her toys. Lucy was overjoyed. From that day on, she always treated her toys well and took great care of them.

Lucy never was quite sure whether the whole thing was a dream or not, but it certainly did the trick, whatever it was. There was one thing that really puzzled her though. If it had just been a dream, why were all the toys so shiny and new again?

Dino's

Menu
Dino's Chips
Caveman's Lunch
Surprise Dish of the Day!

There's a prehistoric venue that is open all day and night. It's the place where dinosaurs meet to catch up on the news, and have a bite to eat. But a bite for a dinosaur is rather large!

Dino's Downtown Diner is full to bursting with large, noisy dinosaurs. The triceratops call in to try the Diplodocus Dips, and pterodactyls leave the sky for Dino's Famous Chips. Raptors are enraptured by the tasty Deep-Fried Lizard. There's Stegosaurus Steak and Brontosaurus Brunch, a massive Mammoth Milkshake and a three course Caveman's Lunch. The plates are huge and are laden with hot and tasty food.

A word of warning though, in case you were thinking of visiting Dino's Downtown Diner one night. They have an extra special dish which, if you join the queue, might not be your idea of fun. Why? Because it's YOU!

Monsters Everywhere

You can find monsters everywhere, if you know where to look! In the jungles and the valleys, in the cupboard under the stairs, in the bedroom and the kitchen – they are lurking everywhere.

In any lake, or pond or puddle, anywhere that fishes swim, you can be sure that lurking there is something rather grim. If you trek up the highest craggy mountain where the snow lies all year long, and listen to the silence you can hear the yeti's song. And if you gaze up into the sky at night, into the depths of the starry twilight, you might just glimpse a UFO. It could be from outer space, a traveller in time zooming towards earth to visit us. Hidden in the depths of the pyramids there are monsters galore, but beware! If you wake a sleeping mummy, it might come chasing after you!

But don't let this talk of monsters make you think it isn't safe to go out anywhere. A monster is part of our imagination. We can make them as horrible and revolting as we like! No one knows if they really exist, do they?

Tiggy-Touchwood

Tiggy-tiggy-touchwood,
   my black hen,
     She lays eggs for gentlemen.
Sometimes nine and sometimes ten,
   Tiggy-tiggy-touchwood,
     my black hen.

I Had a Little Hen

I had a little hen, the prettiest ever seen,
   She washed me the dishes, and kept the house clean;
She went to the mill to fetch me some flour,
   She brought it home in less than an hour;
She baked me my bread, she brewed me my ale,
   She sat by the fire and told many a fine tale.

Sunshine

A sunshiny shower
   Won't last half an hour.

Mrs Hen

Chook, chook, chook, chook, chook,
   Good morning, Mrs Hen.
How many chickens have you got?
   Madam, I've got ten.

Four of them are yellow,
   And four of them are brown,
And two of them are speckled red,
   The nicest in the town.

I Had a Little Cow

I had a little cow;
　Hey-diddle, ho-diddle!
I had a little cow, and it had a little calf;
　Hey-diddle, ho-diddle; and there's my song half.

I had a little cow;
　Hey-diddle, ho-diddle!
I had a little cow, and I drove it to the stall;
　Hey-diddle, ho-diddle; and there's my song all!

Thaw

Over the land freckled with snow half-thawed
　The speculating rooks at their nests cawed
And saw from elm-tops, delicate as flower of grass,
　What we below could not see, winter pass.

The Shortest Tongue Twister

Peggy Babcock

Little Boy Blue

Little Boy Blue,
　Come blow your horn,
The sheep's in the meadow,
　The cow's in the corn.

Where is the boy
　Who looks after the sheep?
He's under a haycock
　Fast asleep.

Will you wake him?
　No, not I,
For if I do,
　He's sure to cry.

Fairy Fern

Deep in the heart of Rosebud Forest lives a tiny little fairy, with beautiful cobweb wings and a magic wand. The fairy's name is Fern, and her home is among the wild flowers that grow in a secret glade.

Fern has a special friend – Sapphire the bluebird. They love to fly through the forest, leaping over rays of sunlight, chasing pretty butterflies. Then, by the light of the moon, Sapphire and Fern dance and sing around a "fairy ring" with all their friends.

Today, Fairy Fern is really excited! There's to be a fairy parade. Flora, the Fairy Queen, will choose the prettiest fairy dress.

FAIRY FERN

With a tap-tap of her wand, Fern magically changes into a dress of velvety rose petals and bluebells. Then, with a sprinkling of fairy dust, Fern makes a secret wish...

"Please let Queen Flora choose me!" she whispers.

But Fern has forgotten to get her friend ready! She weaves some flowers through Sapphire's feathers and adds a sprinkling of fairy dust.

Now for the final touch! Fairy Fern twists her hair up and pins it into place with a golden flower. Then, with a flutter of wings, they fly off to the parade.

Fairy Fern arrives just as Queen Flora is announcing the winner... "and the Golden Crown goes to... Fairy Fern!"

All the fairies cheer and flutter their wings. Fairy Fern smiles as the crown is placed on her head. She is the happiest fairy in the forest — her secret wish has come true.

The Ugly Duckling

Once upon a time, there was a mother duck who laid a clutch of six beautiful little eggs. One day, she looked into her nest in amazement. For there were her six small eggs but lying next to them was another egg that was much, much bigger than the others. "That's odd," she thought, and went back to sitting on the nest.

Soon, one by one, the smaller eggs hatched, and out came six pretty yellow ducklings. Yet the bigger egg still had not hatched.

The mother duck sat on the large egg for another day and another night until eventually the egg cracked, and out tumbled a seventh duckling.

But this one was very different. He was big, with scruffy grey feathers and large brown feet.

"You do look different from my other chicks," exclaimed the mother duck, "but never mind. I'm sure you've got a heart of gold." And she cuddled him to her with all the other ducklings. Sure enough, he was very sweet-natured and happily played alongside the other ducklings.

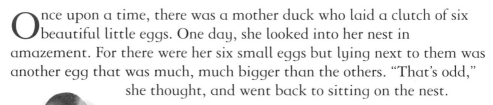

One day, the mother duck led her ducklings down to the river to learn to swim. One by one they jumped into the water and splashed about. But when the big grey duckling leaped into the water he swam

beautifully. He could swim faster and further than any of his brothers or sisters. The other ducklings were jealous and began to resent him.

"You're a big ugly duckling," they hissed at him. "You don't belong here." And when their mother wasn't looking they chased him right away.

The ugly duckling felt very sad as he waddled away across the fields. "I know I'm not fluffy and golden like my brothers and sisters," he said to himself. "I may have scruffy grey feathers and big brown feet, but I'm just as good as they are – and I'm better at swimming!" He sat down under a bush and started to cry. Just then he heard the sound of a dog. Only a short way from where he was hiding, a dog rushed past him, sniffing the ground. The ugly duckling did not dare to move. He stayed under the bush until it was dark and only then did he feel it was safe to come out.

He set off, not knowing which way he was going until eventually, through the darkness, he saw a light shining. The light came from a cosy-looking cottage. The ugly duckling looked inside cautiously. He could see a fire burning in the hearth and sitting by the fire was an old woman with a hen and a cat.

"Come in, little duckling," said the old woman. "You are welcome to stay here."

The ugly duckling was glad to warm himself by the fire. When the old lady had gone to bed, the hen and the cat cornered the duckling.

"Can you lay eggs?" enquired the hen.

"No," replied the duckling.

"Can you catch mice?" demanded the cat.

"No," replied the miserable duckling.

"Well, you're no use then, are you?" they sneered.

The next day, the old woman scolded the duckling: "You've been here a whole day and not one egg! You're no use, are you?"

So the ugly duckling waddled off out of the cottage. "I know when I'm not wanted," he said to himself mournfully.

He wandered along for a very long time until at last he reached a lake where he could live without anyone to bother him. He lived on the lake for many months. Gradually the days got shorter and the nights longer. The wind blew the leaves off the trees. Winter came and the weather turned bitterly cold. The lake froze over and the ugly duckling shivered under the reeds at the lake's edge. He was desperately cold, hungry and lonely, but he had nowhere else to go.

At last spring came, the weather got warmer and the ice on the lake melted. The ugly duckling felt the sun on his feathers. "I think I'll go for a swim," he thought. He swam right out into the middle of the lake, where the water was as clear as a mirror. He looked down at his reflection in the water and stared and stared. Staring back at him was a beautiful white bird with a long, elegant neck. "I'm no longer an ugly duckling," he said to himself, "but what am I?"

At that moment three big white birds just like himself flew towards him and landed on the lake. They swam right up to him and one of them said, "You are the handsomest swan that we have ever seen. Would you care to join us?"

"So that's what I am – I'm a swan," thought the bird that had been an ugly duckling. "I would love to join you," he said to the other swans. "Am I really a swan?" he asked, not quite believing it could be true.

"Of course you are!" replied the others. "You're just like us!"

The three older swans became his best friends and the ugly duckling, that was now a beautiful swan, swam across the lake with them and there they lived together. He knew that he was one of them and that he would never be lonely again.

Princess Petal

Princess Petal lives in a shiny white castle surrounded by beautiful gardens, filled with pretty flowers and colourful butterflies. The Princess's best friend is Sparkle, a sweet little puppy. Every morning, he helps the princess to chose her dress.

"Which one today?" she asks.

Sparkle stands next to a pretty yellow one, wags his tail and barks.

"Perfect," says the Princess.

Then they play games in the garden. They love to run and jump and play "catch the ball".

PRINCESS PETAL

Today, Princess Petal is very excited. She has just received an invitation to a special party – a ball at the palace.

"The Prince is very handsome," Petal says to her puppy. "I must look my best."

She slips on a beautiful pink dress, trimmed with jewels and satin ribbons. On her feet are dainty gold slippers. Then Petal opens her jewellery box and takes out a pair of crystal earrings and a diamond tiara.

She places the tiara carefully on her head – now she can go off to the ball in her beautiful horse-drawn carriage.

As the Princess and Sparkle enter the crowded ballroom, everyone gasps in delight. The handsome Prince takes the Princess's hand.

"You are the loveliest lady here," he says. "May I have this dance?"

"Of course, Your Majesty!" says the Princess.

Princess Petal is the happiest girl in the whole kingdom.

The Red Daffodil

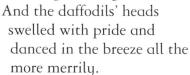

It was spring time and all the daffodils were pushing their heads up towards the warmth of the sun. Slowly, their golden petals unfolded to let their yellow trumpets dance in the breeze. One particular field of daffodils was a blaze of gold like all the others – but right in the middle was a single splash of red. For there in the middle was a red daffodil.

From the moment she opened her petals, the red daffodil knew she was different from the other flowers. They sneered at her and whispered to each other. "What a strange, poor creature!" said one.

"She must envy our beautiful golden colour," said another.

And indeed it was true. The red daffodil wished very much that she was like the others. Instead of being proud of her red petals, she was ashamed and hung her head low. "What's wrong with me?" she thought. "Why aren't there any other red daffodils in the field?"

Passers-by stopped to admire the field of beautiful daffodils. "What a wonderful sight!" they exclaimed. And the daffodils' heads swelled with pride and danced in the breeze all the more merrily.

Then someone spotted the red daffodil right in the middle

of the field. "Look at that extraordinary flower!" the man shouted. Everyone peered into the centre of the field.

"You're right," said someone else, "there's a red daffodil in the middle." Soon a crowd had gathered, all pointing at the red daffodil.

She could feel herself blushing even redder at the attention. "How I wish my petals would close up again," she said to herself in anguish. But, try as she might, her fine red trumpet stood out for all to see.

Now, in the crowd of people gathered at the edge of the field was a little girl. People were pushing and shoving and she couldn't see anything at all. At last, her father lifted her high up on his shoulders so that she could see into the field. "Oh!" exclaimed the little girl in a very big voice. "So that's the red daffodil. I think it's really beautiful. What a lucky daffodil to be so different."

And, do you know, other people heard what the little girl said and they began to whisper to each other, "Well, I must say, I actually thought myself it was rather pretty, you know." Before long, people were praising the daffodil's beauty and saying it must be a very special flower. The red daffodil heard what the crowd was saying. Now she was blushing with pride and held her head as high as all the other daffodils in the field.

The other daffodils were furious. "What a foolish crowd," said one indignantly. "We are the beautiful ones!" They turned their heads away from the red daffodil and ignored her. She began to feel unhappy again.

By now word had spread far and wide about the amazing red daffodil and people came from all over the land to see her.

Soon, the king's daughter got to hear about the red daffodil. "I must see this for myself," said the princess. She set off with her servants, and eventually they came to the field where the red daffodil grew. When the princess saw her, she clapped her hands and jumped up and down with excitement.

"The red daffodil is more beautiful than I ever imagined," she cried. Then she had an idea. "Please bring my pet dove," she said to her servant. The man looked rather puzzled, but soon he returned with the bird. "As you know," said the princess to the servant, "I am to be married tomorrow and I would dearly love to have that red daffodil in my wedding bouquet."

The princess sent the dove into the middle of the field and it gently picked up the daffodil in its beak and brought her back to where the princess stood. The princess carried the daffodil back to the palace. She put the daffodil in a vase of water and there she stayed until the next day.

In the morning, the princess's servant took the red daffodil to the church. The daffodil could hear the bells and see all the guests assembling for the wedding ceremony. Then she saw the princess arrive in a gorgeous coach pulled by four white horses.

How lovely the princess looked in her beautiful gown and her head crowned with deep red roses.

As the servant reached the church door, the princess's lady-in-waiting stepped forward holding a huge bouquet of flowers. Just as the flowers were handed to the princess the servant placed the red daffodil among the other flowers in the bouquet. For a while, the red daffodil was overcome by the powerful scents of the other flowers in the bouquet, but when at last she looked around her she realised, with astonishment, that all of them were red. There were red daisies, red lilies, red carnations and red foxgloves. "Welcome," said one of the daisies, "you're one of us." And, for the first time in her life, the red daffodil felt really at home.

After the wedding, the princess scattered the flowers from her bouquet among the flowers in her garden. Every spring, when she opened her petals, the red daffodil found she was surrounded by lots of other red flowers, and she lived happily in the garden for many, many years.

Witches
on the
Run

At night, when it's all dark and scary, as you peek out over the bed covers, you might see shapes on the wall that will give you a fright! The thought of witches high on the ceiling, with broomsticks, pointed hats and capes can keep you awake all night.

If you think about it for too long, it just gets worse – you can hear their ear-piercing cackles and screams, and the bubbling of their cauldron. If you look really hard, you can see the cauldron glowing with a strange light as the witches cast their spells. They stir the dreadful mixture with a huge wooden spoon, adding slimy green bits. And as you lie there shaking, the smell from the spell gets stronger and the bubbling gets louder!

But there is one thing on the planet that all real witches hate, and that is anything that is clean, particularly clean children! Of course witches never wash, and the thought of children with clean skin makes them feel very ill. They much prefer to be smelly and grimy.

So, the next time you think there are witches flying on your ceiling, remember all you need is clean skin and they will vanish as quick as a flash!

Lonely Hearts

A lonely troll was feeling very depressed one day, and decided that he had to find a mate.

Although this was a good idea, it gave the troll a problem — where does a troll go to find a mate? After thinking for ages he decided the best thing to do was to advertise for someone in the local paper. This is what he wrote:

Fun-loving troll, dirty and smelly,
   With damp slimy skin and big hairy belly
Nice muddy fingers and grubby wet toes,
   Hot steamy breath and rings through each nose.
With stains on his shirt and holes in his socks,
   Teeth that need cleaning and knots in his locks,
Tears in his trousers and scuffs on his shoe,
   He's waiting to meet someone lovely like you.
He likes dirty ditches and hiding in holes,
   Is certain to win when he fights other trolls.
Is very attentive, will woo you with roses,
   After he's used them to pick both his noses!
He lives on his own, in a dark stinking pit,
   Oozing with slime and covered in spit.
Now feeling lonely, he hopes there's a chance
   He can meet someone similar for fun and romance!

Do you know anyone who will reply?

Okey Cokey

You put your left arm in, your left arm out,
  In, out, in, out, you shake it all about,
You do the okey cokey, and you turn around,
  And that's what it's all about.

Oh, the okey cokey,
  Oh, the okey cokey,
Oh, the okey cokey,
  Knees bend, arms stretch,
Ra, ra, ra!

Billy and Me

One, two, three,
  I love coffee,
And Billy loves tea,
  How good you be,
One two three,
  I love coffee,
And Billy loves tea.

Little Nag

I had a little nag
  That trotted up
    and down;
I bridled him, and saddled
    him,
  And trotted out of town.

Mousie

Mousie comes a-creeping, creeping.
  Mousie comes a-peeping, peeping.
Mousie says, "I'd like to stay,
  But I haven't time today."
Mousie pops into his hole
  And says, "ACHOO!
I've caught a cold!"

Mrs Mason's Basin

Mrs Mason bought a basin,
  Mrs Tyson said, "What a nice one,"
"What did it cost?" asked Mrs Frost,
  "Half a crown," said Mrs Brown,
"Did it indeed," said Mrs Reed,
  "It did for certain," said Mrs Burton.
Then Mrs Nix, up to her tricks,
  Threw the basin on the bricks.

Ride a Cock-horse

Ride a cock-horse to Banbury Cross,
  To see a fine lady ride on a white horse,
Rings on her fingers and bells on her toes,
  She shall have music wherever she goes.

These are Grandma's Glasses

These are Grandma's glasses,
  This is Grandma's hat;
Grandma claps her hands like this,
  And rests them in her lap.

These are Grandpa's glasses,
  This is Grandpa's hat;
Grandpa folds his arms like this,
  And has a little nap.

Tickly, Tickly

Tickly, tickly, on your knee,
  If you laugh, you don't love me.

Little Miss Muffet

Little Miss Muffet
  Sat on a tuffet,
Eating her curds and whey;
  There came a big spider,
Who sat down beside her,
  And frightened Miss Muffet away.

Build a House with Five Bricks

Build a house with five bricks,
  One, two, three, four, five.
Put a roof on top,
  And a chimney too,
Where the wind blows through!

Morag
the
Witch

Morag was just an ordinary witch – until the day she enrolled for
a course of advanced spell casting at the Wizard, Witch and
Warlock Institute of Magic. For that was where she met Professor
Fizzlestick. Now Professor Fizzlestick was a very wise old man indeed.
Morag, on the other hand, was a very vain young witch who didn't know
as much as she thought she did. She could turn people into frogs if they
really deserved it, and do other simple spells like that, but she still had a
lot to learn. The problem was, Morag thought she was the most perfect
little witch in the whole wide world.

MORAG THE WITCH

Morag's adventure started on her very first day at school. At the beginning of the day, after all the young witches and wizards had made friends and met the teachers, they were called in one by one to talk to Professor Fizzlestick.

"Now, young Morag Bendlebaum, I taught both your mother and your father," said the professor in a very serious voice, "and a very fine witch and wizard they turned out to be, too. So, what kind of witch do you think you are going to be?"

Without giving this any thought at all, Morag blurted out, "I'm better than my parents, and I'm probably better than you!"

This answer surprised even Morag, for although she thought this was true, she didn't actually mean to say it.

"Don't be surprised by your answers," said Professor Fizzlestick, "there is a truth spell in this room, and whatever you truly believe you must say. And I have to say that you appear to have an enormously high opinion of yourself. Why don't you tell me what makes you so very good?"

"I'm clever," said Morag, "and I'm good, and I'm always right."

"But what about your dark side?" said Professor Fizzlestick.

"I'm sorry to disappoint you," replied Morag quite seriously, "but I'm afraid I simply don't have a dark side."

"Well in that case I would like you to meet someone very close to you," said Professor Fizzlestick with a smile on his lips.

Morag looked over to where Professor Fizzlestick pointed, and was startled to see on the sofa next to her... herself!

As Morag stared open-mouthed with astonishment, the professor explained that if, as she believed, she was without a dark side, then there was absolutely nothing to worry about. "If, however," he continued, "you have deceived yourself, then I'm afraid you are in for a few surprises."

With that the professor dismissed them both from the room and told them to get to know each other. As Morag and her dark side stood outside the professor's room, Morag's dark side jumped and whooped for joy.

"At last," she cried, "I'm free. I don't have to sit and listen to you telling me what's right all day;

I don't have to keep persuading you to
choose the biggest slice of cake before your
brother – in fact, I don't, I repeat don't, have to do
anything that you tell me, at all."

So saying, she broke into a run and rushed down the corridor,
knocking over chairs and bumping into other little witches and
wizards along the way. Morag was horrified. She would have to
follow her dark side and stop her from causing trouble. Morag
chased after her dark side and finally caught up with her at
the chocolate machine. "Don't eat all that chocolate," cried
Morag. "You know it's bad for your teeth and will ruin
your appetite for lunch!"

"Tsk!" scoffed her dark side. "You might not want
any chocolate but I certainly do!" And with that she
ran off once more, dropping chocolate on to the
freshly polished floor as well as pushing a big piece
into her mouth.

Just then, the bell sounded for lunch. Although
Morag felt she ought to find her dark side, she also
knew that the bell was a command to go to the
dining hall, and she mustn't disobey it. Morag sat
down to lunch next to her friend, Topaz. She was just
about to tell her what had happened, when she saw
that Topaz was not eating her vegetables! Morag scolded Topaz for
this, and gave her a lecture on eating healthily.

Topaz stared at Morag in amazement, then peered closely at her.
"What's happened to you?" she asked.

Morag explained what had happened in Professor Fizzlestick's office, and then declared, "And you know, it's the best thing that has ever happened to me. I thought I was good before, but now I'm even better. I never want my dark side back again, but we must find her and lock her up so that she can do no harm."

Topaz agreed that they must find her dark side, but secretly hoped that she and Morag would be reunited. Morag wasn't Morag without her dark side.

After lunch, Morag went for her first lesson of the afternoon. When she walked into the classroom she discovered her dark side already there, busy preparing spells! Morag's dark side had already prepared a "turning a nose into an elephant's trunk" spell and a "turning skin into dragons' scales" spell and was just finishing off a "turning your teacher into stone" spell!

Morag suddenly heard a trumpeting noise from the back of the classroom. She turned to find that the wizard twins, Denzil and Dorian Dillydally, had both sprouted huge grey trunks down to the ground where their noses had been. Morag rushed over to her dark side to make her change them back, but before she could reach her she tripped over a creature crouching down on the floor. It looked just like a dragon and it was wearing a purple and white spotted dress last seen on Bettina Bumblebag. Morag's dark side was casting spells all over the place. "Oh, why doesn't the teacher stop her!" cried Morag to Topaz.

I'm sure you've guessed by now. Nice Miss Chuckle was entirely turned to stone from head to foot!

Just then Professor Fizzlestick walked into the classroom. Morag pointed to her dark side, still making spells at the front of the classroom.

"Lock her up immediately," Morag begged the professor.

"I'm afraid that you are the only one who can do that," said the wise old man. "The two of you are inseparable and you need each other. Without your dark side you would be unbearable and without you she is dreadful. Have I your permission to lock her back inside you?"

Even though Morag didn't want any part of her dark side back, she agreed reluctantly. Her dark side instantly disappeared, and Morag felt... wonderful! Oh, it was so good to be back to normal, to be basically good, but occasionally mischievous.

"Thank you," said Morag to the professor. "I think I've learned something very valuable today."

"There is good and bad in everyone," replied the professor, "even the most perfect of witches."

Morag blushed when she remembered what she had said earlier that morning. Then she realised that she was so relieved to find she was normal that she really didn't mind. Morag and Topaz went back to the classroom to undo all the bad things Morag's dark side had done, but on the way they both felt a huge urge for a snack, so they stopped at the chocolate machine first!

Sleepy the Farm Kitten

Sleepy, the farm kitten, was always tired. He liked nothing better than sleeping all day long, and all through the night. While all the other kittens were busy chasing mice or scaring away birds, he was normally fast asleep.

"Looks too much like hard work to me," he'd yawn, before strolling off to find a comfy spot for a snooze.

One day, while the other kittens were chasing mice around the corn shed, Sleepy stretched and looked around for somewhere to nap.

"You can't sleep here," said the farmer's wife, sweeping Sleepy out of the kitchen. "Today's cleaning day and you'll just be in the way."

"You can't sleep here," clucked the hens, flapping him out of the chicken run. "We're laying eggs and we certainly don't want you watching."

"You can't sleep here," mooed the cows, shooing him out of the milking shed. "We're busy being milked, and a kitten can never be trusted around milk."

"You can't sleep here," said the farmer, pushing him out of the dairy. "We're making ice cream and we don't want your hairs all over the place."

"I'm really tired," Sleepy complained to a passing mouse. "Can I sleep with you mice?"

"Don't be ridiculous," laughed the mouse. "Don't you know that kittens are supposed to chase mice?"

Just as Sleepy was about to give up hope of ever finding somewhere to sleep, he spotted the ideal bed – a soft bale of hay sitting on a trailer.

"Purrfect," he purred, curling into a sleepy ball. Within seconds, he was purring away in his sleep.

He was so comfortable, that he didn't even wake up when the tractor pulling the trailer chugged into life. And he still didn't wake up when the tractor and trailer bumped down the road leading to town.

It was only when the trailer shuddered to a halt that Sleepy woke with a start. He blinked his eyes sleepily, stretched, and looked around. Then he flew to his feet. He couldn't believe his eyes. He was at market and the farmer was driving away in the tractor.

"Wait for me," meowed Sleepy, leaping down from the trailer. But the farmer had gone. "Looks like I'll have to walk all the way home," moaned Sleepy, as he started to walk back towards the farm.

Sleepy walked all afternoon and all through the night. The cockerel was just beginning to crow the morning in when he eventually made it back to the farm.

"Hello, lazybones," called the other kittens when they saw him. "Where have you been sleeping all night while we've been chasing mice?"

But for once Sleepy really was tired – far too tired to explain where he had been all night. And it wasn't long before he was fast asleep!

A Hat Like That

Heather the cow took great care of her appearance. She had the shiniest hooves and the glossiest coat. She had already won three rosettes at the County Show, and she wanted to win more.

One windy afternoon, when Heather was standing near a hedge, she found a beautiful straw hat on a branch. It had a couple of holes in it, but an elegant cow has to put her ears somewhere!

She strolled back across the field with her nose in the air, and the hat placed firmly on her head. Heather couldn't wait to show it off to her friends.

But Poppy, Annabel and Emily simply carried on munching. Heather tried a tiny ladylike cough. The munching didn't stop for a second. So Heather coughed a little louder. The munching grew louder.

Heather couldn't bear it any longer. "Haven't you noticed it?" she mooed.

"Did I hear something?" asked Emily.

"It was me!" cried Heather, stamping her hoof crossly.

"Oh, so it was," said Annabel, and returned to a particularly juicy clump of green grass.

"Oh dear! I'm feeling rather sleepy, I think I'll just have a little snooze," said Poppy.

"And I'm going for a walk," said Emily.

Heather was not a patient cow. "Look at my hat!" she cried.

Of course, the other cows had noticed the hat, but they loved to tease their friend.

"I always think," said Poppy, "that hats are rather… old-fashioned."

"Nonsense," Heather replied. "Only the most fashionable cows are wearing them."

"It's new then, is it?" asked Annabel.

"Certainly!" Heather replied. "It's the very latest style."

"Didn't Mrs MacDonald have a hat like that a few years ago?" asked Emily.

"I don't think so!" Heather said firmly. "Mrs MacDonald is lovely, but she's not what you would call stylish. Only a prize-winning cow could carry off a hat like this."

"If you say so, dear," mooed Annabel.

That evening, the cows ambled into the farmyard to be milked. Before long, all the other animals had gathered round.

"They're admiring my hat!" whispered Heather to Poppy.

But the giggling and chuckling didn't sound as if they thought Heather looked beautiful. It sounded more like animals who thought she looked rather silly.

"Well, well! So that's what happened to Scarecrow Sam's hat!" cried Old MacDonald.

Nowadays, if Heather starts putting on airs and graces, Poppy, Emily and Annabel know just what to do — they start talking about hats, and Heather tiptoes away.

Grandma Elephant's Birthday

"Boris," said his parents, "it's a special day today. Can you remember why?" They say elephants never forget, but Boris never remembered. He wrinkled his forehead and thought very hard.

"Do I start school today?" he said. "Is it my birthday?" asked Boris.

"Getting closer," said Mum. "It's Grandma Elephant's birthday! I want you to take her this basket of fruit. Can you remember where she lives?"

"Yes," nodded Boris. Mum gave him the basket and watched him leave.

Boris walked through the forest. It was very quiet and shady. "Boo!" shouted a voice suddenly. Boris looked round and saw a very strange animal. It looked like a mouse with wings. "Do I know you?" asked Boris.

"I'm Fruit Bat, ninny," said the fruit bat.

"What do fruit bats do?" asked Boris.

"Eat fruit, of course," said the bat. "Where are you off to?"

"It's Grandma Elephant's birthday, but I can't remember how to get to her house," said Boris.

"If I tell you, will you give me some fruit?" asked the bat. Boris nodded. "That's the path over there," pointed the bat, taking an apple from Boris's basket.

The path was very narrow. Right in the middle, blocking the way, was a huge gorilla.

"I'm taking fruit to Grandma," said Boris bravely. "It's her birthday."

"Don't you remember who I am?" asked Gorilla.

"You're Rhinoceros," Boris guessed.

"If you can't remember who I am," said Gorilla, "you'll have to give me some fruit!" Boris couldn't remember so Gorilla took two bananas and let Boris pass.

Reaching a crossroads, Boris didn't know which path to take. "Take the left path," said a voice high above him. Looking up, Boris saw Giraffe with his head sticking out of the top of a tree. "Are you going to Grandma Elephant's? I can see her house from up here," said Giraffe.

"Thank you," said Boris. "Have some fruit!"

"That's very kind of you," said Giraffe. He took a pear from the basket.

When Boris arrived at Grandma's house, all that was left in the basket was one juicy plum! What would Grandma say? Would she be cross? He needn't have worried. Grandma hugged him and took him to the kitchen.

There, sitting round the table, were Fruit Bat, Gorilla and Giraffe, all wearing party hats. In the middle of the table was a big birthday cake, a large wobbly red jelly, and all the fruit from Boris's basket.

Grandma said it was the nicest birthday she could remember.

Boris couldn't remember the way home. So when the party was over his friends took him all the way back. His mum was so pleased to see him.

"Aren't you going to introduce me to your friends?" she asked.

"This is Bat Fruit, Crocodile and Giraffe," said Boris.

Everybody laughed. Silly Boris... what a memory!

Monday's Child is Fair of Face

Monday's child is fair of face,
   Tuesday's child is full of grace,
Wednesday's child is full of woe,
   Thursday's child has far to go,
Friday's child is loving and giving,
   Saturday's child works hard for his living,
And the child that is born on the Sabbath day
Is bonny and blithe, and good and gay.

Little Jumping Joan

Here am I, little jumping Joan.
   When nobody's with me,
I'm always alone.

There Was a Little Girl

There was a little girl, and she had a little curl
   Right in the middle of her forehead;
When she was good she was very, very good,
   But when she was bad she was horrid.

Anna Maria

Anna Maria she sat on the fire;
   The fire was too hot, she sat on the pot;
The pot was too round, she sat on the ground;
   The ground was too flat, she sat on the cat;
The cat ran away with Maria on her back.

A Pretty Little Girl in a Round-eared Cap

A pretty little girl in a round-eared cap
   I met in the streets the other day;
She gave me such a thump,
   That my heart it went bump;
I thought I should have fainted away!
   I thought I should have fainted away!

Goldy Locks, Goldy Locks

Goldy locks, goldy locks,
   Wilt thou be mine?
Thou shall not wash dishes,
   Nor yet feed the swine;

But sit on a cushion,
   And sew a fine seam,
And feed upon strawberries,
   Sugar and cream.

Mr Punchinello

Oh! mother, I shall be married
   To Mr Punchinello.
   To Mr Punch,
   To Mr Joe,
   To Mr Nell,
   To Mr Lo,
   Mr Punch, Mr Joe,
   Mr Nell, Mr Lo,
   To Mr Punchinello.

Gilly Silly Jarter

Gilly Silly Jarter,
   Who has lost a garter?
In a shower of rain,
   The miller found it,
The miller ground it,
   And the miller gave it
To Silly again.

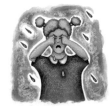

The Naughty Mermaids

Of all the mermaids that lived in the sea, Jazz and Cassandra were the naughtiest. They were not supposed to swim above sea when there were people about. But their latest prank was to swim to the lighthouse and call out to the little boy, Jack, who lived there.

"Coo-ee," they would call and, when the little boy looked towards them, they giggled and dived under the waves. When King Neptune heard about it, he was very cross indeed!

One day, Jack's mum made him a picnic. Jack laid the food on a cloth on the rocks. He had pizza and crisps and fizzy drink and chocolate.

The two naughty mermaids popped up from the waves and saw all the food. "Hello!" they called to Jack. "Are you going to eat all this food by yourself?" Jack was surprised, he'd never seen the mermaids before.

"Yes," said Jack. "I mean, no! You can have some of my picnic, if you like." The mermaids had never had pizza or crisps or fizzy drink or chocolate before. They ate so much they felt sick! They swam home slowly, hoping King Neptune wouldn't spot them. But he did, and he summoned them to see him.

"Be warned!" said King Neptune. "Mermaids are not

like children. They cannot behave like children and they cannot eat the food that children eat!"

For a while Jazz and Cassandra ate mermaid food, like shrimps and seaweed, but they soon became bored. "I'm longing for some pizza," said Jazz to Cassandra one day.

"So am I," answered Cassandra, "and some crisps, and chocolate!" Then the naughty mermaids swam up to the surface.

Jack was there with another picnic. The mermaids ate everything, then they played hide and seek in the waves while Jack ran round the lighthouse trying to spot them. The mermaids enjoyed themselves so much, they came back the next day and the next. On the third day, the mermaids said goodbye and started to swim to the bottom of the sea. But, oh dear! Their tails had become stiff and heavy. They could not move! King Neptune was right. Mermaids can't behave like children. They clung on to the rocks around the lighthouse and began to cry.

"What's wrong?" shouted Jack, alarmed. "We're not supposed to eat children's food," they told him. Jack knew exactly what to do! He got his net and bucket and collected shrimps and seaweed from the rock pools.

For three days and three nights he fed the mermaids proper mermaid food. By the third day they could move their tails again and swim.

When they arrived home King Neptune was waiting for them.

This time, King Neptune wasn't angry – he was glad to see them back safely. "I hope you have learned a lesson," he said, quite gently. "Jack has been a good friend so you can play with him again. As long as you don't eat his food!"

Fancy Flying

Penelope Parrot and her mum, Portia, were having a wonderful afternoon, watching the Fancy Flying Display Team. Penelope could hardly believe her eyes as she saw the birds swoop and speed through the sky, doing their amazing tricks and wonderful stunts.

That night, Penelope dreamt about doing magnificent stunts with the other birds and, in the morning, she decided she would try to make her dream come true!

"I'm going to practise flying, Mum," she said. "I want to be the best!" Before Portia could say a word, Penelope had zoomed off.

"The first thing I have to do is learn to fly really fast," Penelope told herself. So she flapped her wings as hard as she could, to get up some speed. But Penelope had only just learned to fly – so she didn't know how fast or how far she could go. Soon she was huffing and puffing and panting, and her wings were flopping instead of flapping! "Oh, nooooo!" she cried, as she felt herself falling down… down… down… until… SPLASH! She landed right beside Howard Hippo, who had been enjoying his morning wallow. "Gracious, Penelope," said Howard, trying to shake the water out of his eyes and ears. "You must be more careful!"

"Sorry, Howard," said Penelope. "I didn't plan that. I was just seeing how fast I could fly and my wings got tired. I want to be a Fancy Flyer!"

"Then you'll need expert help," said Howard.

"But I don't know any experts," said Penelope.

"But I do," came a voice from the bank. It was her mum, Portia. "I've been trying to find you to tell you some special news," said her mum. "My uncle Percy has just arrived for a visit. He was a member of the original Fancy Flying team! He can give you the training you need."

Uncle Percy was delighted to hear that Penelope wanted to be a Fancy Flyer. "I'll teach you lots of stunts first," he said, "and then we'll work on one that will be your very own. Every Fancy Flyer has a speciality!"

Uncle Percy and Penelope went right out to start her training programme.

"We'll begin with the Twisting Take Off," Uncle Percy said. "Watch me and do as I do."

"Now, straighten up and fly forward!" Percy called. But Penelope couldn't stop spinning and spinning!

"Whoa!" she shouted. "I'm getting dizzy, Uncle Percy!"

Luckily, Penelope grabbed a branch and managed to stop spinning.

Jeremy Giraffe, who was nibbling leaves nearby, helped Penelope up as Uncle Percy flew back.

"Never mind," said Uncle Percy. "You'll soon get the hang of it."

Just then, Penelope's friends, Mickey, Maxine and Chico, came swinging by.

"Want to play Mango-Catch with us?" they called.

"Great!" said Penelope, flying over to join them.

"Wait!" said Uncle Percy. "A Fancy Flyer in training can't waste her energy on games!"

"Sorry, Uncle Percy," said Penelope. "I guess I'll see you all later," she said, a little sadly.

"In fact," said Uncle Percy, "I think it's time you were in your roost."

"But Uncle Percy," Penelope said, dismayed, "it's so early!"

"A Fancy Flyer needs her sleep, my dear!" said Uncle Percy. "Those wing muscles need lots of rest to prepare for all the work they must do."

"Better do what Uncle Percy says," said Portia, as she helped Penelope settle on to her bedtime branch. "He's the expert!"

The next morning, Uncle Percy woke Penelope up very early. "Time for your pre-dawn practice!" he squawked.

"But Uncle Percy, it's so early!" Penelope yawned. "The sun's not even up yet!"

"That's the best time to train!" said Uncle Percy. "Follow me!"

"We'll start with some speed exercises," Uncle Percy said. "This was my speciality when I was a Fancy Flyer. Just move in and out through the trees – like this!"

Penelope watched her uncle weave gracefully through the jungle. It looked easy, but when she tried…

THUH-WHACK! "Ouch!" cried Penelope.

Uncle Percy came rushing back to look at Penelope's head. "Nothing serious," he said. "A Fancy Flyer in training has to expect a few bumps and bruises! Best thing to do is keep going. Let's try it again."

All day, Uncle Percy tried to teach Penelope stunts. And all day, Penelope bashed… and crashed… and smashed… and splashed… into trees and other animals!

It was a very tired and worn-out Penelope who headed for home with Uncle Percy that afternoon.

"Well, Penelope," said Portia, when the two arrived back, "are you ready to be a Fancy Flyer?"

"Oh, yes," said Penelope. "And I know exactly what my speciality will be!"

"What?" asked Portia and Uncle Percy together.

"Watching from the audience!" laughed Penelope.

The Tale of Two Princesses

Long ago there were twin princesses called Charmina and Charlotte. Even though they were twins, they were opposites. Princess Charmina was gracious and charming to everyone. She curtsied politely to the king and queen. And she remained quite still while the dressmakers came to fit her new ball gown. Princess Charlotte was very different!

"Why do I have to dress like a puffball?" grumbled Princess Charlotte when it was her turn to have a new ball gown fitted.

"How dare you speak to us like that!" her parents cried. But she did dare. She dared to run barefoot through the gardens until her hair looked like a bush. She dared to wear her shabbiest clothes. In fact, she didn't behave like a princess at all!

One day there was to be a ball at the palace. The guests of honour were two princes from the next kingdom. The two princesses, dressed in their new ball gowns, kept getting in the way of the preparations. "Why don't you go for a walk until our guests arrive," suggested the queen. "But stay together, don't get dirty and don't be late!"

The two princesses walked to the bottom of the palace gardens. "Let's go into the forest," said Princess Charlotte.

"I don't think we should," said Princess Charmina. "Our gowns will get dirty." But Princess Charlotte had already set off.

"I think we should go back," Princess Charmina told her sister. "We'll be late for the ball." Just then they heard a strange noise. "Let's turn back!" said Princess Charmina.

"It may be someone in distress!" said Princess Charlotte. "We must go and help!" Although Princess Charmina was scared she agreed. "But we must get back in time for the ball."

They set off again going even deeper into the forest. Finally, they came upon two horses in a clearing, but there was no sign of their riders. Just then they heard voices calling out, "Who's there?"

At first, the two princesses couldn't see where the voices were coming from. In the middle of the clearing there was a large pit. They peered over the edge. Princess Charmina stared in astonishment. Princess Charlotte burst out laughing. There at the bottom of the pit were two princes.

"Well, don't just stand there," said the princes. "Help us out!"

The two princesses found ropes and threw one end down to the princes. They tied the other end to the horses. Soon the princes were rescued.

On their return they found the king and queen furious that their daughters had returned late looking so dirty. But their anger turned to joy when the two princes explained what had happened.

Everyone enjoyed the ball. The two princesses danced all night with the two princes. From that time on, Charlotte paid more attention to her gowns and hair. And Charmina became a little more playful and daring than before!

You're Not My Best Friend

Gabriella Goat, Chicken Charlotte, Sam the Sheepdog, Penfold Pig, Sally the Sheep and Jersey Cow all lived on Willow Farm. In the late afternoon when all the farm work had been done, they liked to meet in the paddock next to the farmyard to talk.

Gabriella was a very self-important goat, because she thought she was more useful on the farm than all the other animals. Not only did she provide milk for the farmer's wife to make cheese, but she also nibbled all the nettles and weeds and kept the farmyard neat and tidy. As far as she was concerned, that was much more important than just laying eggs or looking after sheep, or helping the farmer look for truffles, growing wool, or making milk.

Each morning, when Chicken Charlotte had finished laying eggs and all the other animals were still hard at work, she would flutter over the picket fence that kept the foxes away and strut over to visit Gabriella.

YOU'RE NOT MY BEST FRIEND

One very hot day when the sun was shining down on the garden, Gabriella decided she and Chicken Charlotte should go down to the duck pond and soak their feet in the clear, cool water. Chicken Charlotte didn't like this idea at all! "I'm afraid I might fall in and drown," said Chicken Charlotte. "I can't swim."

"You can't swim?" gasped Gabriella Goat. "How can you be any fun if you can't swim?" And she turned her back on Chicken Charlotte. Gabriella thought about who liked swimming, then she smiled. "Sam the Sheepdog can swim," she said. "Sam will be my very best friend."

Sam the Sheepdog had just finished chasing Sally the Sheep into the field when Gabriella Goat called out to him, "How about taking a break now and coming to the duck pond with me?"

"Why not?" Sam asked when he'd got his breath back. "It's a boiling hot day and I could do with a nice long swim to help me cool down."

Gabriella and Sam had tremendous fun all day splashing around in the water, and at the end of the day Gabriella said to Sam, "You're my very best friend. Let's do this again tomorrow!"

Sam agreed. He was delighted that Gabriella liked him the best of all the animals.

The next day, Gabriella went to fetch Sam so that they could play. Sam was in the field chasing Sally but, when Gabriella beckoned for him to come and play, Sam shook his head. "It's too early," said Sam. "I've got to make sure Sally grazes all this field, and the pond is all muddy now. The farmer won't like it if I get too dirty."

"What?" squealed Gabriella Goat in disbelief. "Whoever heard of a dog that didn't like mud?" And with that she turned her back on Sam the Sheepdog. Gabriella thought for a while about who else might like mud, and then smiled triumphantly. "Penfold Pig likes getting muddy," she said. "Penfold Pig will be my very best friend."

Penfold Pig was snuffling around in the hot yard when Gabriella Goat found him. "Come and roll in the mud with me," said Gabriella.

They had such fun that Penfold wanted to do this again the following day, but Gabriella said that she'd had enough of basking now, and tomorrow she wanted to lie in the field and chew juicy grass. Penfold Pig was distraught. He didn't like chewing grass – he liked pig-swill. Sadly, he told Gabriella Goat that he'd not be able to join her.

"You'll never make a good best friend if you can't eat grass," huffed Gabriella. And with that she turned her back on Penfold Pig. She thought about who else liked eating grass, and then smiled triumphantly. "Jersey Cow likes eating grass," thought Gabriella Goat. "Jersey Cow will be my very best friend."

The following morning, Gabriella went to find Jersey Cow, who was just about to be milked by the farmer's wife. She told Jersey Cow her plans for the day. Jersey Cow said that she would be honoured to have Gabriella to talk to as they chomped and lazed the day away. "I'll be with you in just a tick," said Jersey Cow. "I need to be milked first."

Gabriella Goat stared at Jersey Cow, and then turned and walked away! "What's wrong with all these silly animals?" she asked herself. "Why do they have to do something else first, or can't even do something at all?" And with that she decided to go alone to the juicy green field.

When Gabriella got to the field, she spied Sally the Sheep grazing away. Sally the Sheep was very pleased to be chosen as Gabriella's friend, and they spent the next hour talking and munching away. Before very long, Jersey Cow came to join them.

"Friendship is all about giving and taking," remarked Gabriella to Sally the Sheep (so that Jersey Cow could overhear), "and being a very best friend means giving a lot." But, when Jersey Cow moved off to chew some grass a little further away, Sally the Sheep followed her. Gabriella Goat snorted in disgust, and then chewed some more. "Who needs friends anyway?" she thought. "They're no good to anyone."

Gabriella Goat started to feel bored. She wanted to play a game. All the animals were together in the paddock. But, when Gabriella got close, all the animals turned their backs.

Just then she heard Jersey Cow remark to Sally the Sheep, "You know, friendship is all about giving and taking. If a friend of mine wouldn't give as well as take, she'd be no friend of mine."

Gabriella was very upset. She skulked off to the farmyard and was utterly miserable. The more she thought, the more miserable she became. The more miserable she became, the more she realised what a terrible friend she had been. The next day when she saw all her former friends, she sobbed, "I'm so sorry, won't you all forgive me?"

Chicken Charlotte flew to her side and gave her a big hug, and then all the other animals joined in. Nobody had liked seeing her so sad, and they all wanted to be friends again. "I've been so silly," said Gabriella, "but now I realise that you are ALL my very best friends."

Oh, Bear!

Mr Bruin's
Big Top Circus

Bear and Rabbit had been shopping. There were posters all over town about the circus that was coming.

"I think I might join the circus," said Bear, as they reached his gate.

"What would you do?" asked Rabbit.

"I'd walk the tightrope," said Bear. "It's easy peasy." And he leapt on to the clothes line. He began well. He glided gracefully. He somersaulted superbly. He bowed beautifully. Then disaster struck! He wavered and wobbled. He teetered and tottered. He lost his grip and began to slip…

"Oh, Bear!" laughed Rabbit.

"Oh, well," said Bear, as he picked himself up. "Perhaps I'll ride a unicycle instead."

"But you haven't got a unicycle," said Rabbit.

"I can fix that," said Bear. And he disappeared into his shed. Soon, Rabbit heard tools clanging and banging.

"There," called Bear, as he cycled out of the shed. He began quite well. He pedalled up and down. He pirouetted round and round. Then disaster struck!

OH, BEAR!

"Oh, Bear!" laughed Rabbit, as he watched Bear get tangled and the cycle get mangled.

"Oh, well," said Bear, as he picked himself up. "Perhaps I'll juggle instead."

"But there's nothing to juggle," said Rabbit.

"I'll find something," said Bear. And he disappeared into the kitchen. Rabbit waited patiently. He heard crockery clinking and clattering.

"There," said Bear, as he juggled down the path. He began quite well. He whirled the cups and twirled the plates. Higher and higher they went. Then disaster struck! The cups and plates crashed and the whole lot smashed.

"Oh, Bear!" laughed Rabbit.

"I'm not sure the circus is a good idea," Rabbit told Bear.

"Nonsense!" said Bear. "Of course it is."

"But Bear," said Rabbit. "You've tried walking the tightrope. You've tried riding a unicycle. You've tried juggling. And look what happened."

"Yes," said Bear. "Look what happened. I made you laugh. Now I know exactly the right job for me," and quickly he ran indoors.

It wasn't long before he was back.

"Oh, Bear!" laughed Rabbit. "You're right. You make a perfect clown!"

The Broom Song

Here's a large one for the lady,
　Here's a small one for the baby;
Come buy, my pretty lady,
　Come buy o' me a broom.

Chairs to Mend

If I'd as much money as I could spend,
　I never would cry, "Old chairs to mend.
Old chairs to mend! Old chairs to mend!"
　I never would cry, "Old chairs to mend!"

My Maid Mary

My maid Mary,
　She minds the dairy,
While I go a-hoeing and mowing each morn;
　Merrily runs the reel,
And the little spinning wheel,
　Whilst I am singing and mowing my corn.

The Gossips

Miss One, Two, and Three
　Could never agree,
While they gossiped around
　A tea-caddy.

Cock-crow

The cock's on the wood pile
　Blowing his horn,
The bull's in the barn
　A-threshing the corn,
The maids in the meadow
　Are making hay,
The ducks in the river
　Are swimming away.

Puss in the Pantry

Hie, hie, says Anthony,
　Puss is in the pantry,
Gnawing, gnawing,
　A mutton, mutton bone;
See how she tumbles it,
　See how she mumbles it,
See how she tosses
　The mutton, mutton bone.

Buff

I had a dog
　Whose name was Buff,
I sent him for
　A bag of snuff;
He broke the bag
　And spilt the stuff,
And that was all
　My penny's worth.

Puss at the Door

Who's that ringing at my door bell?
  A little pussycat that isn't very well.
Rub its little nose with a little mutton fat,
  That's the best cure for a little pussycat.

Grig's Pig

  Grandpa Grig
  Had a pig,
In a field of clover;
  Piggy died,
  Grandpa cried,
And all the fun was over.

Three Ghostesses

Three little ghostesses,
  Sitting on postesses,
Eating buttered toastesses,
  Greasing their fistesses,
Up to their wristesses.
  Oh what beastesses
To make such feastesses!

Washing Day

The old woman must stand
  At the tub, tub, tub,
The dirty clothes to rub, rub, rub;
But when they are clean,
  And fit to be seen,
She'll dress like a lady
  And dance on the green.

Cock Robin's Courtship

Cock Robin got up early
  At the break of day,
And went to Jenny's window
  To sing a roundelay.
He sang Cock Robin's love
  To little Jenny Wren,
And when he got unto the end
  Then he began again.

Engine, Engine

Engine, engine, number nine,
  Sliding down Chicago line;
When she's polished she will shine,
  Engine, engine, number nine.

Thank You

Thank you for your portrait,
  I think it's very nice.
I've put it in the attic
  To scare away the mice.

Elsie Elephant's Jungle Shower

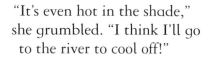

U p above the jungle there wasn't a cloud in the sky. Deep down inside the jungle Elsie Elephant was feeling very hot.

"It's even hot in the shade," she grumbled. "I think I'll go to the river to cool off!"

Tommy Monkey was swinging high up in the tree-tops. "I'm going swimming," Elsie told him. "You can come too, if you like." Tommy jumped out of the tree and skipped along with Elsie.

"You've got a very long trunk," said Tommy Monkey.

"What is it for?"

Elsie thought about it for a minute. "I'm not really sure," she said at last.

At the river they found Leo Lion standing at the edge of the water, looking in. "Hello Leo – are you coming for a swim?" asked Elsie.

"Lions don't like swimming," sighed Leo. "But I'm so hot! I'll come and watch you."

Soon Stripy Tiger arrived. She and Leo watched as Elsie and Tommy Monkey dived into the river and began splashing around.

"It's lovely and cold – jump in!" shouted Elsie.

"Tigers are a bit scared of water," called Stripy. "But it does look fun!"

Elsie saw how hot all her friends looked and had an idea. She filled her trunk with cool water and sprayed it all over Leo Lion and Stripy Tiger. Soon Tommy Monkey and even the jungle birds came to play under Elsie's shower.

"NOW I know what my long trunk is for!" said Elsie happily, and all the animals cheered!

Maria's Haircut

One spring day, Maria the sheep stood by the pond in Old MacDonald's farmyard, gazing sadly into the water.

"What is she doing?" whispered Doris the duck to her friend Dora. "You don't often see sheep near water."

Meanwhile, ducklings were swimming across to see who the visitor was.

"Sheep don't eat ducklings, do they?" asked Dora, anxiously. She was not a clever duck!

"Of course not!" replied Doris. "They are quite safe with Maria."

But, just then, Maria gave such a big sigh that she blew the ducklings right across the pond and they had to be rescued by their mothers!

Old George the horse couldn't bear to see another animal on the farm feeling unhappy. He clip-clopped across the yard and rubbed his big head against Maria's woolly back. "What's the trouble, my dear?" he asked. "Has your lamb run away again?"

"No," sighed Maria. "It isn't that. Just look at me!"

Old George looked carefully at Maria. "Well, you look even more, er, wonderfully woolly than usual," he said, gallantly.

"I look a fright," said Maria. "My coat should have been trimmed weeks ago, but Old MacDonald seems to have forgotten."

"Hmmmm. He can be a little forgetful," said Old George. "I'll speak to the other animals and see what they suggest."

The animals were most interested in Maria's problem. "Perhaps I could nibble her coat," said Percy the pig, who would eat almost anything! A general chorus of disapproval greeted this idea.

"No, we must remind Old MacDonald to give Maria a haircut," said Poppy the cow.

"Old MacDonald is always so busy," added Henrietta the hen. "I don't know how we can make him notice Maria's problem!"

And that gave Poppy a very good idea. "No," she mooed, "it's Mrs MacDonald that notices things. Perhaps you should do some nibbling after all, Percy."

So, Percy did a little nibbling, then the hens scurried away with the tufts of wool in their beaks, and determined looks on their faces, searching for the farmer.

When Old MacDonald went into the farmhouse for his lunch that day, Mrs MacDonald threw up her hands in horror!

"MacD!" she cried. "You're covered in wool! Don't bring all those fluffy bits into my clean kitchen! It's obviously time those sheep were shorn."

The very next day, Maria's haircut was the talk of the farmyard.
And she and her friends strutted happily around, looking as smart and
as stylish as any sheep you've ever seen.

Sugarplum and the Butterfly

"Sugarplum," said the Fairy Queen, "I've got a very important job for you to do." Sugarplum was always given the most important work. The Fairy Queen said it was because she was the kindest and most helpful of all the fairies. "I want you to make a rose-petal ball gown for my birthday ball next week."

"It will be my pleasure," said Sugarplum happily.

Sugarplum began to gather cobwebs for the thread, and rose petals for the dress. While she was collecting the thread she found a butterfly caught in a cobweb.

"Oh, you poor thing," sighed Sugarplum. Very carefully, Sugarplum untangled the butterfly, but his wing was broken. Sugarplum laid the butterfly on a bed of feathers, then she gathered some nectar from a special flower and fed him a drop at a time. Then she set about mending his wing with a magic spell.

After six days, the butterfly was better. He was very grateful. But now Sugarplum was behind with her work!

"Oh dear! I shall never finish the Fairy Queen's ball gown by tomorrow," she cried. "Whatever shall I do?" The butterfly comforted her.

"Don't worry, Sugarplum," he said. "We'll help you."

He gathered all his friends together. There were yellow, blue, red and brown butterflies. He told them how Sugarplum had rescued him from the cobweb and helped to mend his wing.

The butterflies gladly gathered up lots of rose petals and dropped them next to Sugarplum. Then the butterflies flew away to gather more cobwebs, while Sugarplum arranged all the petals. Back and forth went Sugarplum's hand with her needle and thread making the finest cobweb stitches. Sugarplum added satin ribbons and bows. When she had finished, Sugarplum was very pleased.

"Dear friend," she said to the butterfly, "I couldn't have finished the dress without your help."

"And I could never have flown again without your kindness and help," said the butterfly.

The Fairy Queen was delighted with her new ball gown. And, when she heard the butterfly's story, she wrote a special Thank You poem for Sugarplum:

Sugarplum is helpful,
   Sugarplum is kind.
Sugarplum works hard all day,
   But she doesn't mind.
She always does her
    very best,
   To make sick creatures
    well.
She brings such joy
   and pleasure
   As she weaves her
    magic spell!

The Funny Bunny

The Funny Bunny's in a flap.
　He'll never get it done!
Every year, it's just the same.
　He's such a hot, cross bun!

When everyone is fast asleep,
　He hops off to the farm,
Clutching an enormous list,
　His basket on his arm!

He taps upon the hen house door.
　He hopes that they've been busy.
The hens laugh at his worried face.
　He's always in a tizzy!

They fill his basket to the brim,
　With eggs of every hue.
There's brown and white
　　and speckled ones
　And some are even blue!

"Now, off you go," they cluck at him.
　"And mind that they don't break.
You've just time to deliver them,
　Before they're all awake!"

He stops to peer at his long list,
　Then hops up to a door.
There's two for here and one for there
　And next door, they need four!

The busy bunny hops and skips,
　All round and round the towns,
To make quite sure the children wake
　With smiles and not with frowns!

Then, suddenly, the sun wakes up.
　The cock crows, "Hey! It's dawn."
"At last, my job is finished!"
　Sighs the bunny, with a yawn!

But what is this? There's one egg left.
　He checks his list to see
If anyone has been left out.
　"Oh, yes!" he smiles. "It's me!"

Bertha Saves the Day

Bertha Bunny had a shiny nose,
　But this she could not mend,
Because her little powder puff
　Was at the other end!

She felt upset, because her chums
　All chuckled at the sight
Of Bertha's pink and perky nose,
　That shone just like a light!

One day, the bunnies hopped
　and skipped
　And wandered off to play
Too far into the Wicked Wood,
　Then couldn't find their way!

"Oh, no! We're lost!" sobbed Little Bob,
　Because he's only three.
"My mummy will be worrying
　If I'm not home for tea!"

It got so dark, they couldn't tell
　Just which way they should go.
Then, Bertie spotted Bertha's nose,
　All shiny and aglow!

"Bertha's nose will light our way!"
　Cried Bertie Bun, with glee.
"Yippeeee!" the other
　　bunnies yelled.
　"We'll soon be home for tea!"

They followed Bertha through
　　the wood.
　"You're such a clever bunny,"
Said Billy, as they got back home.
　"And your nose isn't funny!"

"Without it, we would
　　all be lost
　Forever in the wood.
Three cheers for Bertha's
　　shiny nose.
　We think it's really good!"

103

Mummy's Having a Baby

Josh was helping his mum to do the washing-up. "Guess what, Josh?" said Mum. "Soon, you're going to have a baby brother or sister to play with." She bent down and wiped some bubbles off his nose.

"Will the baby look like me?" asked Josh.

Mum laughed. "Oh, I hope so," she said. "Now, you'll have to help me. We've got *lots* to do before baby arrives."

The very next day, Josh and his mum went shopping. They chose some stripy baby-grows, a furry teddy bear and a brand new car seat – *all* for the baby! "What about *me?*" thought Josh.

Just then, Mum gave Josh a present. "Here you are," she said. "Thanks for helping me."

"Thanks, Mum!" cried Josh.

When they got home, Dad had brought Josh's old cot and buggy down from the attic. Josh lay in the buggy and ate his tea.

MUMMY'S HAVING A BABY

"But what about *me?*" he said, sadly. "That's *my* cot."

"You don't need this any more," laughed Dad. "You're a big boy now." Josh smiled.

As the weeks went by, Josh waited… and waited… and waited! Was this baby *ever* going to arrive? Then, one day, Mum said, "I'm going to the hospital, Josh. I think baby is coming today."

"But what about *me?*" asked Josh.

"Don't worry," said Mum. "Granny is here to look after you."

"I love Granny, but I don't want you to go," sniffed Josh. "I'll miss you."

"I'll miss you, too," said Mum and she hugged him tightly. "Don't worry. I'll be back soon."

Later that day, Dad came home from the hospital. "Josh!" he called. "You've got a beautiful baby sister. Come on, I'll take you to meet her. We've called her Molly." When they got to the hospital Dad took lots of photos – of baby Molly!

"What about *me?*" grumbled Josh, quietly. He was feeling left out.

Then, Dad said, "Let's have a picture of Josh and Molly together." He took the photo… then another… and another! Josh felt much better.

When Mum and Molly came home, lots of friends came to visit. They all wanted to see Josh's sister and they brought lots

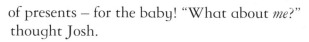

of presents – for the baby! "What about *me?*" thought Josh.

"Look what Molly has bought for you," said Mum. And there, in Molly's cot, was a big parcel, tied up with a bow.

"Thanks for my train," said Josh and he gave his sister a big kiss.

Little babies take a lot of looking after! Molly always seemed to be hungry and her nappy needed changing a lot! She liked being cuddled, too. "What about me?" thought Josh. "Will someone cuddle me, please!"

When Dad came home, he scooped Josh up and cuddled him. "I need a hug, too," said Dad. "Who will give me one?"

"I will," squealed Josh, laughing.

When they walked in the park, everyone wanted to look at baby Molly. No one seemed to notice Josh, except Mrs Jackson. "Molly looks just like you," she said. Josh smiled, proudly. "I think her nose is like mine," he said. Mum was getting tired.

"Looking after Molly is very hard work," said Dad.

"What about *me?*" said Josh. "I can help Mum." So, when Molly was upset, Josh pulled funny faces and made his sister laugh. When Molly wanted to play, Josh built brick towers and let her knock them down,

again… and again… and again! And when Molly dropped her rattle, Josh *always* picked it up for her.

At the supermarket, Mum let Josh push the buggy, which made him very happy. Everyone stopped to talk to him and his sister. "You really *are* Mummy's little helper, aren't you, Josh?" they said. And Josh was the only one who could get Molly off to sleep. He sang all his favourite songs to her. With Josh's help, Mum had more time to spare.

"Who wants a story and a nice, big cuddle?" she asked, sitting on the sofa.

"I do," laughed Josh. Mum started to read a story. Suddenly, Josh asked, "What about Molly? Can she hear the story, too?"

"Of course, she can," laughed Mum and went to fetch her. Then, Mum started to read again.

"What about *me*?" asked Dad, as he sat on the sofa. "Can I listen?"

"Of course, you can," laughed Josh. "Molly and I want *everyone* to join in."

Lazy Mary

Lazy Mary will you get up,
　　Will you get up, will you get up?
Lazy Mary will you get up,
　　Will you get up today?

　　Six o'clock and you're still sleeping,
　　　　Daylight's creeping o'er your windowsill.

Lazy Mary will you get up,
　　Will you get up, will you get up?
Lazy Mary will you get up,
　　Will you get up today?

Seven o'clock and you're still snoring,
　　Sunshine's pouring through your window pane.

Lazy Mary will you get up,
　　Will you get up, will you get up?
Lazy Mary will you get up,
　　Will you get up today?

Eight o'clock, you've missed your train,
　　Can you explain why you're still in your bed?

Little Betty Blue

Little Betty Blue
Lost a holiday shoe,
What can little Betty do?
Give her another
To match the other,
And then she may
　　swagger in two.

Anna Banana

Anna Banana
　　Played the piano;
The piano broke
　　And Anna choked.

See-saw, Margery Daw

See-saw, Margery Daw,
　　Johnny shall have a new master;
He shall have but a penny a day,
　　Because he can't work any faster.

Lucy Locket

Lucy Locket lost her pocket,
  Kitty Fisher found it.
Not a penny was there in it,
  Only ribbon round it.

Cinderella's umbrella's
  Full of holes all over.
Every time it starts to rain
  She has to run for cover.

Aladdin's lamp is getting damp,
  And is no longer gleaming.
It doesn't spark within the dark,
  But you can't stop it steaming.

Here Comes a Widow

Here comes a widow from Barbary-land,
  With all her children in her hand;
One can brew, and one can bake,
  And one can make a wedding-cake.
Pray take one, pray take two,
  Pray take one that pleases you.

Elsie Marley

Elsie Marley is grown so fine,
  She won't get up to serve the swine,
But lies in bed till eight or nine,
  And surely she does take her time.

Mary, Mary, Quite Contrary

Mary, Mary, quite contrary,
  How does your garden grow?
With silver bells, and cockle shells,
  And pretty maids all in a row.

The Elves and the Shoemaker

Once upon a time there was a kind old shoemaker who lived in a tiny flat above his shop with his wife. He had many bills to pay, so he had to work from dawn to dusk to pay them off. The day came when he had only a few pennies left – just enough to buy leather for one final pair of shoes.

That evening, by candlelight, the shoemaker cut up the leather. Then, leaving it on his workbench, he picked up his candle and wearily climbed the stairs to his bed.

The next morning, when he came down to his shop, the shoemaker could not believe his eyes. There on his workbench, where the leather had been, was the finest pair of shoes he had ever seen.

The shoemaker went to the stairs and called to his wife to come and see what he had found. "Did you make these shoes?" he asked her.

"Of course not," she replied.

The shoemaker was very puzzled and

scratched his head in amazement. "Then who could it have been?" he wondered.

The shoemaker put the shoes in his shop window. That afternoon, a fine gentleman came to try them on. He liked the shoes very much, and gave the shoemaker a good price for them.

With the money, the shoemaker was able to buy food for dinner, and had enough left over to buy leather to make two new pairs of shoes.

Later that night, the shoemaker cut up the leather and left it lying on his workbench. "I'll finish the shoes in the morning," he yawned, shutting up the shop. He picked up the candle and went up the stairs to bed.

The next morning, when he came downstairs, the shoemaker was truly amazed. There, sitting neatly on his workbench, were two fine pairs of beautiful new shoes! They were soft and delicate. He thought they were the best shoes he had ever seen.

Once again, the shoemaker called his wife and asked if she had made them. "Oh, husband," she said, "of course I didn't."

The shoemaker was confused, but once again he put them in his shop window, where everyone could see them. In no time at all, he had sold both pairs for a very good price.

That evening, the shoemaker and his wife had a marvellous dinner. There was also enough money left to buy leather to make four new pairs of shoes!

Once more, the shoemaker cut out the leather and left it neatly on his workbench. And, in the morning, there were more new shoes waiting for him when he came downstairs.

So it went on for weeks. Every night the shoemaker cut out the leather and left it on his workbench, and every morning there were splendid shoes waiting to be sold.

Soon the shoemaker and his wife were quite wealthy. But they still did not know who was making the smart shoes that appeared in the shop as if by magic.

One cold, wintry night, just before Christmas, the shoemaker and his wife decided that they had to solve the mystery once and for all. So, after the shoemaker left the leather on his workbench, he shut

up the shop and hid in a big cupboard with his wife. They left the door slightly open so that they could see, and waited… and waited… and waited.

At last, when the clock struck midnight, there was a tiny noise from the dark chimney. It grew louder. Suddenly, two tiny elves appeared in a shower of magical stars. They ran straight over to the workbench and began to stitch and sew, until they had made five beautiful pairs of shoes.

They sang as they worked:

"There isn't any time to lose,
We must make these fine new shoes!"

As soon as the shoes were finished, they hopped off the workbench and shot up the chimney. The shoemaker and his wife were amazed.

The shoemaker and his wife wanted to do something in return for the kind little elves. What could they do?

"They must be frozen in those thin, tattered clothes," said the shoemaker.

"Yes," said his wife. "And their feet are bare, although they make such beautiful shoes!"

So the shoemaker's wife made two little jackets and two pairs of trousers. She knitted four little woolly socks to keep their feet warm, and two tiny hats for their heads. The shoemaker made two pairs of small boots, fastened with shiny silver buckles.

That evening, they wrapped the little clothes in tissue paper and left them on the workbench. Then they hid in the cupboard and waited for the elves.

At the stroke of midnight, there was a noise from the chimney and the elves appeared in the shower of magical stars. They were puzzled when they saw parcels instead of leather. But, when they opened all the presents, they were overjoyed. They quickly put on their new clothes and danced happily all around the shop. As they danced they sang,

"See what handsome boys we are!
We will work on shoes no more!"

They danced happily across the room, flew up the chimney and were gone in a flash!

The elves did not return, but the man and his wife never forgot the two tiny men and all their hard work.

The shoemaker continued to make shoes which were fine and beautiful, and he became rich and famous across the land. But none compared to the beautiful, light and delicate shoes that the little elves had made!

Kiss It Better

Rumpus was romping around the living
room. He cartwheeled across the carpet. He turned a somersault on
the sofa. "Be careful!" called Mum.

Too late! Rumpus slipped from the sofa,
crumpled on to the carpet and banged his
head on the floor. "My head hurts!"
he groaned.

"Come here and I'll kiss it better," said
Mum. She hugged Rumpus and planted a
kiss on his forehead. "Now, go and find
something less rowdy to do," she said.

Rumpus rushed
out into the
garden and began
to ride his bike. Round and
round he raced. "Watch out!" called Mum.

Too late! Rumpus crashed into the corner
of the wheelbarrow and tumbled to the
ground and grazed his knee. "My leg
hurts!" he wailed.

"Come here and I'll kiss it better," said
Mum. She hugged Rumpus and planted a
kiss on his knee.

KISS IT BETTER

"Now, go and find something safer to do," she said.

Rumpus ran up the grassy slope. Then he rolled down. "Roly poly, down the hill," he sang. "Look where you're going!" called Mum.

Too late! Rumpus rolled right into the rose bush. The thorns scratched him all along his arm. "My arm's sore!" cried Rumpus.

"Come here and I'll kiss it better," said Mum, and she planted kisses all up his arm.

"Now, try and keep out of trouble," she said.

Mum went into the kitchen. "I need a break," she thought. She made a cup of tea. She cut herself a slice of cake. Then, she sat down for five minutes. Just as she picked up her cup, Rumpus zoomed into the kitchen on his skateboard.

"Rumpus!" said Mum. "Can't you find something more sensible to do?" Mum moved into the living room. "I need a rest," she thought. She sat down on the sofa and picked up the paper.

"Boom! Boom! Boom!" In marched Rumpus, banging on his drum. Mum sighed a loud sigh. "Is anything wrong?" asked Rumpus.

"I've got a headache!" said Mum.

"Never mind," smiled Rumpus, throwing his arms around her. "I'll soon kiss it better."

The Greedy Hamster

There was once a hamster named Harry. He was a very greedy hamster. As soon as his food was put in his cage he gobbled it all up, and then he would push his little nose through the bars in the hope that something else to eat might come within reach. From his cage he could see all manner of delicious food on the kitchen table – and the smells! The scent of freshly baked bread was enough to send him spinning round in his exercise wheel with frustration.

"It's not fair!" he grumbled to himself. "They're all eating themselves silly out there and here am I simply starving to death!" (At this point he would usually remember the large meal he had just eaten and that his tummy was indeed still rather full.)

"If only I could get out of this beastly cage, I could feast on all the food I deserve," he announced to himself, and the thought of all those tasty morsels made his mouth water.

One night after the family had gone to bed, Harry was having one last spin in his wheel before retiring to his sawdust mattress. As he spun around, he heard an unfamiliar squeaky noise.

"That's funny," thought Harry. "The little girl oiled my wheel only today.

It surely can't need oiling again." He stopped running and got off the wheel, but the squeak continued. Harry sat quite still on his haunches and listened intently. Then

he realised it was the door to his cage squeaking. The door! The door was flapping open. The little girl had not closed it properly before she went to bed. Harry did a little dance of glee. Then he went to the door and looked cautiously out in case there was any danger. But all seemed to be well. The cat was asleep on a chair. The dog was sleeping soundly on the floor.

Now, as well as being a greedy hamster, Harry was clever. Once outside the cage, the first thing he did was look at the catch to see how it worked. Yes! He was pretty sure he could work out how to open it from the inside now. Harry sniffed the air. There were some tasty titbits left over from a birthday party on the table. He could smell the sugar icing, and soon he was on the table, cramming his mouth with odds and ends of cheese sandwiches and pieces of chocolate cake. When he had eaten his fill, he stuffed his cheek pouches with ginger biscuits and ran back into his cage, closing the door behind him.

"Good!" thought Harry. "Now I will never be hungry again."

The next night Harry let himself out of his cage and helped himself to food, and again the next night and the night after that.

He feasted on everything and anything – nuts, bananas, pieces of bread, left-over jelly and slices of pizza were all pushed into his greedy mouth. Each time he returned to his cage he filled his cheeks with more and more food. He did not notice that he was getting fatter and fatter, although he was aware that he could no longer run round in his wheel without falling off! Then, one night, he undid the door catch but found he was simply too wide to get through the door!

For a while Harry sat in a very bad temper in the corner of the cage. His cheeks were still bulging with food from his last midnight feast, but the greedy hamster wanted more. Then he had an idea. "I'll get that lazy cat to help," he thought. He squealed at the top of his voice until the cat, who had been dreaming of rats, woke up with a start.

"What do you want?" she hissed at Harry. Harry explained his problem.

"Of course, I'd be only too pleased to help," said the crafty cat, thinking to herself here was an extra dinner! With her strong claws she bent back the door frame of the cage, until there was just enough room for Harry to squeeze through. Then, with a mighty swipe of her paw, she caught him and gobbled him whole. She felt extremely full, what with Harry and all his food inside her. She could barely crawl back to her chair and soon she was fast asleep again and snoring loudly with her mouth open. Inside her tummy Harry, too, felt very uncomfortable. Every time the cat snored, it sounded like a thunderstorm raging around his head.

"I must get out of here," he thought, and headed for the cat's open jaws. But he was far too fat to get out again. Then he had another idea. Through the cat's jaws he could see the dog lying on the floor.

"Help! Help!" he squeaked. The dog woke up to a very strange sight. There was the cat lying on the chair snoring, but she also seemed to be squeaking, "Help!" The dog put his head on one side. He was very perplexed. Then he saw a pair of beady eyes and some fine whiskers inside the cat's mouth. It was Harry!

"Get me out of here, please," pleaded Harry.

Now the dog did not very much like the cat, so he was quite willing to help the hamster.

"I'll stick my tail in the cat's mouth. Then you hang on while I pull you out," said the dog. "But mind you don't make a sound and wake the cat, or she'll surely bite my tail!" The dog gingerly put the tip of his tail inside the cat's open jaws, just far enough for Harry's little paws to grab hold. Then he pulled with all his might. Out popped Harry and out of Harry popped all the food he'd stored in his cheeks – peanuts, an apple core and a slice of jam tart!

"Thank you, thank you," gasped Harry as he made a dash for his cage and slammed the door shut. "I think I'll stay in my cage from now on and just eat all the food that I'm given!"

Cuddles to the Rescue

Cuddles was a very smart little poodle. Her hair was snowy white and fell in perfect curls. Her claws were always neatly trimmed and polished. She wore a crisp red bow on top of her head. And she never, ever went out without her sparkly jewelled collar.

Once a week Cuddles was sent to the poodle parlour, where she was given a wash, cut and blow dry. And every morning Gilly, her owner, brushed and styled her hair until she looked exactly like herself.

But although Cuddles was the smartest, most pampered pooch around, she was not happy. You see, she didn't have any doggy friends.

Whenever Gilly took her walking in the park, Cuddles tried her best to make friends but the other dogs didn't want to know her.

"Here comes Miss Snooty," they would bark. Then they'd point and snigger, before racing away to have some playful puppy fun.

And Cuddles was never let off her velvet lead. "Those other dogs look rough," explained Gilly. "You're far safer walking with me."

Cuddles would have loved to run around with the other dogs. She thought that chasing sticks and balls looked like brilliant fun. And she was sure that she'd be able to swim in the lake if only Gilly would let her.

But the other dogs didn't know that Cuddles wanted to be one of them.

They just took one look at her snowy white curls and sparkly collar and thought that she was too posh for them.

"She doesn't want to get her paws dirty," Mrs Collie explained to Skip, her youngest pup, when he asked why Cuddles was always on a lead.

Then one day, Cuddles was walking with Gilly in the park, when she saw Skip chasing ducks beside the lake.

"Careful!" barked Cuddles, as Skip bounced up and down excitedly.

But Skip was far too busy to listen. Then, as a duck took off, Skip took an extra large bounce, and threw himself into the lake.

"Stop!" barked Cuddles. But it was no good, Skip was already up to his chin in water.

"Help, help!" barked Skip, as he splashed about wildly in the lake. Cuddles gave a loud bark, and then, using all her strength, pulled the lead from Gilly's hand.

Cuddles was already in the water. Gilly looked on in horror as Cuddles caught the struggling pup by the scruff of his neck and pulled him ashore.

Once on dry land, Cuddles gave herself a big shake, then started to lick Skip dry.

"Cuddles," breathed Skip, who was quickly recovering from his ordeal.

"Cuddles!" cried Gilly, pointing in horror at her soaking wet curls and muddy paws.

"Will you play with me?" barked Skip, wagging his tail hopefully.

After that, Gilly always let Cuddles play with the other dogs in the park, and Cuddles was the happiest little poodle around.

A Farthing

I went into my grandmother's garden,
    And there I found a farthing.
I went into my next door neighbour's;
    There I bought
A pipkin and a popkin,
    A slipkin and a slopkin,
A nailboard, a sailboard,
    And all for a farthing.

Jack Sprat's Cat

Jack Sprat,
    Had a cat,
It had but one ear;
    It went to buy butter
When butter was dear.

Butterfly

I'm a little butterfly
    Born in a bower,
Christened in a teapot,
    Died in half an hour.

My Little Maid

Hey diddle doubt,
    My candle's out,
My little maid's not at home;
    Saddle the hog,
    And bridle the dog,
And fetch my little maid home.

Home she came, trittity trot,
    She asked for the porridge she left in the pot;
Some she ate, and some she shod,
    And some she gave to the truckler's dog.

In Marble Halls

In marble halls as white as milk,
    Lined with skin as soft as silk;
Within a fountain crystal clear,
    A golden apple doth appear.
No doors there are to this stronghold –
    Yet thieves break in and steal the gold.

Tiddle Liddle

Tiddle liddle lightum,
    Pitch and tar;
Tiddle liddle lightum,
    What's that for?

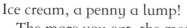

Ice Cream

Ice cream, a penny a lump!
    The more you eat, the more you jump.

The Flying Pig

Dickery, dickery, dare,
  The pig flew up in the air;
The man in brown
  Soon brought him down,
Dickery, dickery, dare.

Four Stiff Standers

Four stiff standers,
  Four dilly-danders,
Two lookers,
  Two crookers,
And a wig-wag!

When the Wind...

When the wind is in the East,
  'tis neither good to man or beast.
When the wind is in the North,
  the skilful fisher goes not forth.
When the wind is in the South,
  it blows the bait in the fish's mouth.
When the wind is in the West,
  then it is at its very best.

Roundabout

Round about, round about,
  Maggoty pie;
My father loves good ale,
  And so do I.

Kindness

If I had a donkey that would not go,
  Would I beat him? Oh no, no.
I'd put him in the barn and give him some corn,
  The best little donkey that ever was born.

A Song

I'll sing you a song,
  Nine verses long,
  For a pin;
Three and three are six,
  And three are nine;
You are a fool,
  And the pin is mine.

Little Friend

In the greenhouse lives a wren,
  Little friend of little men;
When they're good she tells them where
  To find the apple, quince and pear.

Bella Bunny's Bonnet

In pretty Primrose Wood, there was great excitement. It was the Spring Parade. All the animals were joining in because a prize was being given for the best bonnet. "I bet I'll win," said Bella, who was a very vain bunny. "What can I use for my hat?" she wondered, as she skipped through the woods. Bella gathered some pretty Spring flowers, then called her friend, Binky the pigeon, for help. The friends worked hard, weaving daffodils and bluebells into a beautiful display.

"There," said Binky, "perfect." Bella put on the pretty hat and smiled.

"I know I'm going to win!" she cried. Binky just smiled. Bella really was the vainest animal in Primrose Wood! At last, it was time for the parade. The animals from Folly Farm were all wearing jolly bonnets. "There isn't one hat as pretty as mine," giggled Bella. "It looks good enough to eat!" Gordy the goat thought so, too. Trotting behind Bella, he nibbled her bonnet, until he had gobbled up nearly all the flowers!

Then, Holly the horse gave a loud neigh. "The winner of this year's parade is Felicity the fox!" she said.

Everyone cheered – except Bella. "But mine is the best – look!" Bella took the hat off her head. "Aaagghh! My lovely hat!" she cried, looking at a clump of twigs!

"Oops!" said Gordy. "Sorry, Bella."

"But you have won something," sniggered Holly. "The prize for the funniest hat!"

Brave Billy Bunny

At the edge of Frog Pond Wood, there lived a friendly, little bunny called Billy, his brother Bobby and lots of bunny friends. The one thing Billy really, really hated was getting wet! One sunny day, the other bunnies and Bobby hopped off to the stream, to play. "Come on, Billy!" they called.

"No way!" cried Billy. "I hate the water!"

What Billy loved doing most of all was running. So, while the other bunnies played at the stream, Billy ran through the wood, leaping over logs and weaving in and out of the trees – he was very fast! Suddenly, Bouncer Bunny came rushing back from the stream.

"Billy! Come quickly!" he panted. "Bobby's fallen into the water and is being washed away!" Billy rushed off towards the stream, leaving poor Bouncer far behind. When Billy reached the stream, he could just see his little brother, Bobby, splashing away in the rushing water.

"Help!" cried Bobby. "I can't swim!"

Then, Billy began to run! He managed to get ahead of Bobby. Quickly, Billy jumped into the water, swam up to his brother and, coughing and spluttering, dragged poor Bobby to the side.

"Billy!" cried the others. "You're a hero!"

"A wet hero!" said Billy, grinning. "Getting wet wasn't so bad after all. I'm going for another swim!"

Slow Down, Bruce

On Old MacDonald's farm, no one works harder than Bruce the sheepdog – except, of course, Old MacDonald! All day long, Bruce dashes around the farm, keeping an eye on everything that goes on.

It was Bruce who barked to warn the farmer when a branch of the old apple tree was just about to fall on his head!

It was Bruce who found the lambs about to escape through a hole in the hedge!

And it was Bruce who pulled one of Milly's kittens out of the duck pond.

Bruce is on the go from dawn to dusk – he really loves his job!

So, when Bruce stayed in his kennel one morning with his head on his paws, everyone began to worry.

"It's not like him at all," clucked Henrietta the hen.

"He can hardly open his eyes," purred Milly the cat.

"I've never known him have a day's illness in his life," said Old George the horse, "and I remember him as a pup."

Old MacDonald was more worried than any of them.

"Just stay there, old boy," he said gently. "I'll get someone to help you." And he hurried off to call the vet.

The vet arrived very quickly. She too was very fond of Bruce.

She carefully examined him, lifting his paws one by one, and checking every part of him thoroughly. Then she patted the old dog's head and said, "You're like your master. You need to stop dashing around so much and take better care of yourself. You'll be fine in a day or two, but just slow down, Bruce. Take it easy for once, please."

Bruce nodded his head gratefully and went back to sleep.

Now, Mrs MacDonald had been listening, and returned to the farmhouse with a thoughtful look on her face.

Bruce did as he was told, and by the end of the week he was as right as rain – it would soon be time to go back to work.

When he saw Old MacDonald rushing through the yard, hurrying to finish a job, Bruce dashed after him.

But Mrs MacDonald rushed out of the farmhouse and called to the farmer.

"Husband!" she cried. "Did you hear what the vet said about Bruce? You must set him a good example! Please be a little more thoughtful!"

So, Old MacDonald began to slow down, and so did Bruce. The sheepdog soon felt better for it – and so did

Old MacDonald. And Mrs MacDonald, who had been begging her husband to take it easy for years, felt very happy indeed.

Harvey the Shyest Rabbit

Harvey the rabbit was the shyest animal in the glade beside Looking-Glass Pond. He was too shy to talk to anyone... too shy to play with the other animals... too shy even to look out from behind his big floppy ears.

"There's no need to be scared," Mama Rabbit told him. "If you want to join in, all you have to do is ask."

But Harvey just hid behind the long grass. No one even noticed that he was there!

One morning, Harvey was sitting beside Looking-Glass Pond – alone, as usual.

"I wish I could make a friend," he sighed. "But how can I, when no one even notices me?"

Harvey gazed down sadly at the pond. He could hardly believe his eyes! There in the water was another little rabbit with big floppy ears, staring back at him.

"He looks just as scared as me!" thought Harvey. He waved shyly at the rabbit in the water. The water rabbit waved too! Harvey did a bunny hop in surprise. The water rabbit did a bunny hop. "Hello!" said Harvey bravely, smiling.

"Hello!" said the rabbit, smiling back. "So that's how you make friends!" cried Harvey, in amazement. "You just need to be a little bit brave."

He was so excited, he forgot all about being shy or scared. Instead, he raced off to tell everyone the good news.

And this time, everyone noticed him! Soon Harvey had lots of new friends to play with. But he never forgot to visit his very first friend in Looking-Glass Pond!

Small and Pink

One morning, Percy the pig strutted proudly through the farmyard. "Today's the day," he told everyone he passed.

"What is he on about?" asked Doris the duck.

"Percy is expecting some piglets," clucked Jenny the hen.

"I didn't think boy pigs could have babies," said Doris, looking puzzled.

"No, no," Jenny clucked, flapping her wings. "They are coming from another farm to live here as part of his family."

Doris smiled. "Like Tilly and George and their new foal?" she said. "Oh, how lovely."

Percy had tripped and trotted from one end of the farmyard to the other more times than he cared to remember, but Old MacDonald still hadn't returned with the new arrivals.

Percy went back to his sty and checked it one more time. It was spotless. The straw was piled up neatly along one wall and the water trough was clean and full.

"I must make sure that everything is ready for my piglets," said Percy, brushing a speck of dust from the doorway.

Just as Percy finished cleaning, brushing and tidying he heard Old MacDonald's truck rumbling into the farmyard – they were here at last!

Percy was so excited! He hurried from his sty, but before he could reach the truck...

Whoosh! Something very small, very pink and very fast shot past his nose.

Whizzz! Something just as small and pink and even faster scuttled under his tail.

Wheeeee! Another small and pink and noisy thing zoomed straight under Percy's tummy.

"What's going on?" gasped Percy, as he spun round on his trotters.

"Eeeeeeeeee!" shrieked seven little piglets, dashing in every direction around the farmyard.

Late that night, a very tired Percy stood at the doorway of his sty – it was a tip. The straw was everywhere and the water trough was upside down. But seven little piglets were fast asleep in the corner.

"Tired, Percy?" asked Jenny the hen.

"Yes," sighed Percy.

"They never stand still from morning till night, do they?" added Maria the sheep.

"No," sighed Percy.

"Are you having second thoughts, Percy?" asked Old George the horse.

But Percy gave the kind of grin that only a very happy and contented proud pig can give. "Shhhhhhh!" he whispered. "My babies are sleeping!"

Thank You, Kitty

"Come here, Kitty," calls Cat one day. "I've got a surprise for you." Kitty bounces over. "You can have lots of fun with this ball of wool," says Cat. Soon Kitty is laughing and leaping around.

"Watch me, Mum! I can pat the ball into the air," she shouts.

Just then Kitty hears someone calling her. "Kitty," calls Mother Bird. "Please can I have some of your wool for my nest?"

Kitty looks at Cat. "I won't have anything to play with," she says sadly. "It won't be as much fun."

Cat smiles, "It's much more fun to share things, Kitty," she says.

Kitty and Cat watch as Mother Bird tucks the wool into her nest. "The baby birds like the wool don't they, Mum?" laughs Kitty. "I like sharing," says Kitty. "Who else can I share my wool with, Mum?" asks Kitty.

"Why don't you ask the rabbits if they could use some?" says Cat.

"We're having a hopping race," says Little Rabbit. "A piece of wool is just what we need to make a finishing line. Thank you, Kitty."

Just then Cat calls Kitty over. "I have another surprise for you," she says. "It's a bell from Mother Bird," says Cat. "To thank you for sharing your wool."

"What a lovely present," says Kitty. "Would you like to play with it too, Mum?"

You Can Do It, Kitty

It's a lovely day. Kitty and Cat are having fun on the farm. "Climbing trees is fun," says Cat. "Watch me, Kitty."

Cat leaps up the tree. "Where are you, Mum?" calls Kitty.

"Climb up, Kitty," calls Cat. "You'll love it up here."

Kitty runs to the tree. But then she starts to cry. "I can't," she sobs. "It's too high."

Cat gives Kitty a snuggle. "Don't be upset," she says. "You can do anything you want to do. You'll soon be at the top of the tree. See that little calf over there, Kitty? He is trying to walk."

"But he cannot even stand up," says Kitty.

"Keep watching," says Cat. "Now he can run and jump."

Then Kitty and Cat see the tree again. Kitty takes a deep breath. "Watch me, Mum! I'm going to do it!" she says.

Kitty runs to the tree and… jumps! "You've done it, Kitty!" shouts Cat.

Kitty hugs Cat. "It's brilliant up here, Mum," she says. "I can see the whole farm."

The Apple Tree

Here is the tree with leaves so green.
   Here are the apples that hang between.
When the wind blows the apples fall.
   Here is a basket to gather them all.

The Cherry Tree

Once I found a cherry stone,
   I put it in the ground,
And when I came to look at it,
   A tiny shoot I found.

The shoot grew up and up each day,
   And soon became a tree.
I picked the rosy cherries then,
   And ate them for my tea.

Here We Go Round the Mulberry Bush

Here we go round the mulberry bush,
   The mulberry bush, the mulberry bush,
Here we go round the mulberry bush,
   On a cold and frosty morning.

This is the way we wash our hands,
   Wash our hands, wash our hands,
This is the way we wash our hands,
   On a cold and frosty morning.

Here we go round the mulberry bush,
   The mulberry bush, the mulberry bush,
Here we go round the mulberry bush,
   On a cold and frosty morning.

This is the way we wash our clothes,
   Wash our clothes, wash our clothes,
This is the way we wash our clothes,
   On a cold and frosty morning.

Here we go round the mulberry bush,
   The mulberry bush, the mulberry bush,
Here we go round the mulberry bush,
   On a cold and frosty morning.

Lavender's Blue

Lavender's blue, dilly, dilly, lavender's green,
  When I am king, dilly, dilly, you shall be queen;
Call up your men, dilly, dilly, set them to work,
  Some to the plough, dilly, dilly, some to the cart;
Some to make hay, dilly, dilly, some to thresh corn;
  Whilst you and I, dilly, dilly, keep ourselves warm.

Dancing Round the Maypole

Dancing round the maypole,
  Dancing all the day,
Dancing round the maypole,
  On the first of May,
Dancing round the maypole,
  What a merry bunch,
Dancing round the maypole,
  Till it's time for lunch.

Dancing round the maypole,
  Shouting out with glee,
Dancing round the maypole,
  Till it's time for tea.
Dancing round the maypole,
  Blue and white and red,
Dancing round the maypole,
  Till it's time for bed.

I Had a Little Nut Tree

I had a little nut tree, nothing would it bear,
  But a silver nutmeg, and a golden pear;
The King of Spain's daughter came to visit me,
  And all for the sake of my little nut tree.
    I skipped over water, I danced over sea,
      And all the birds of the air
        couldn't catch me.

Don't be Shy, Kitty

Kitty is playing with a yo-yo. "Watch me, Mum," she says. "I can make it go up and down." Suddenly, from the farmyard, Kitty hears laughing. "What is it, Mum?" she asks Cat.

"There's a big game going on," says Cat. "It looks fun, doesn't it, Kitty?"

Just then, Parsnip the pig spots Kitty. "Hello, Kitty! Come and join in!" he says. But Kitty hides behind Cat instead.

"What's the matter, Kitty?" asks Cat gently.

"The game is so loud. It makes me feel shy," Kitty says sadly.

"There's no need to be shy," says Cat. "All your friends are here."

But Kitty still feels shy. "I think I'll just watch for a bit," she says. The animals are having a wonderful time.

Then, Dennis the donkey gives the ball a big kick. "Whoops!" says Dennis. "Did anyone see where the ball went?" Quick as a flash, Kitty leaps up and races up the tree.

"I can see the ball, Mum!" she shouts. "Here it is!" Kitty laughs, throwing it down from the tree. "You're a hero, Kitty!" the animals shout. The game starts again and now Kitty is right in the middle of things.

"Great kick, Kitty," shouts Parsnip.

"You were right, Mum," she says. "I didn't need to feel shy at all."

Kitty and Cat Help Out

Kitty and Cat are going for a walk around the farm. "Look at the bees, Kitty," says Cat. "They're very busy." Suddenly Cat hears another noise. "Someone's crying," she says. "What's the matter, Little Rabbit?" asks Cat. "Why are you crying?"

"I've lost my teddy bear," sniffs Little Rabbit. "It's my favourite toy."

"Don't worry," says Kitty. "We'll help you look for it. Perhaps it's behind the haystack. I'm going to look inside the tractor," says Kitty.

"Well, I can't see your teddy," calls Kitty. "But here's my ball of wool!"

Cat points to the gate. "Perhaps you left your teddy in the field, Little Rabbit," she says. Little Rabbit begins to cry again.

"I'll never find my teddy," he wails.

"Don't give up," says Kitty kindly. "I'm sure we'll find it soon."

"Have you looked for your teddy at home, Little Rabbit?" asks Cat. "It could be there, you know. We've looked everywhere else."

So they walk slowly to Little Rabbit's home, carefully looking for teddy on the way. But, when they arrive, they find teddy! He is tucked right down inside Little Rabbit's bed.

Little Rabbit gives Kitty a big hug. "Thank you, Kitty and Cat," he says. "I'd never have found my teddy without you!"

The Rainy Day

Rain! Rain! Rain! It had rained all day at Faraway Farm. It splashed on the windows, gurgled down the drainpipes, and made puddles all over the yard. Big muddy footprints were everywhere. Danny and Rosie's bored faces peered through the window, longing for it to stop.

Out in the pigsty, Bessie and her piglets wallowed in a giant mud bath. It was such fun! There were squeals of delight.

On the pond, the ducks bobbed along looking pleased with themselves. As long as the raindrops kept falling they were happy.

Cosy inside, Conker slept in his basket by the stove and Stan the cat sat on the window sill washing his paws. Rosie drummed her fingers on the window and pressed her forehead against the pane. She sang a little song to herself: "Rain, rain go away. Stop, I want to go and play."

Down by the bridge, the river was rising higher and higher. Eventually, it spilled over its banks and brown muddy water flowed across the road and under the farm gate. The cows all gathered to shelter under an old tree.

Joe was busy fixing the tractor in the barn. He wore bright overalls and stomped round the yard in his big muddy boots. He caught sight of the postman riding his bike up to the farm and waved. The rain still pelted down. All of a sudden there came a shout from the road.

"Help, Joe! I'm stranded by the flood," called Jack, the postman. Joe frowned seeing the poor postman stranded.

"Don't worry, Jack," he shouted back. "We'll soon get you across."

Joe put down his tools and climbed up into the tractor cab. He started the engine and reversed out of the barn. The trailer was hooked on. The windscreen wipers swished to and fro. The water splashed down the sides of the cab.

Rosie and Danny emerged from the house in their waterproofs and ran down to the bridge with Conker. "Look," gasped Rosie. "The ducklings are swimming all over the garden. And Jack the postman's trapped by the flood!"

Joe rumbled up in the tractor. "Get on the trailer," he shouted to the children. "I'll reverse it through the flood." They splashed through the water and climbed on to the wall. Danny helped Rosie and Conker on to the trailer.

"Nice weather for ducks," puffed Jack, as he scrambled aboard. "Thanks, kids. Oh, no! There goes my cap!"

Conker barked wildly and jumped in after it. "Oh, come back, Conker," wailed Rosie. "You'll be swept away in the flood."

"No he won't, silly," said Danny. "He's a champion swimmer. Go fetch it, boy!" Conker grabbed the postman's cap in his mouth, and paddled back to the trailer. He dropped it and wagged his tail expectantly.

"Good old Conker!" shouted everyone. "Well done, boy!" Conker shook himself furiously, spraying them all with water.

Joe drove back to the yard and they all jumped off the trailer. Danny climbed up into the cab and Joe let him switch off the engine.

"Thank you, everyone," said Jack, picking up his cap. "Especially you, Conker. I'm very fond of this old cap."

"Come inside," called Mum. "You're all wet through."

"The letters are a bit damp this morning," said Jack. "So is my cap. But at least I've still got one, thanks to Conker."

"Put it by the kitchen stove to dry out," suggested Mum.

"Brave dog," said Danny, giving Conker a pat.

Jack stood by the stove, warming up and drinking a cup of coffee. "We'll help you with the rest of your round. You can sit on the back of the trailer and Rosie and Danny will help deliver the letters," Joe said kindly. So that's what they did.

"That was fun," said Rosie, when she got home.

"I'm going to be a postman when I grow up," said Danny. "But I'm going to have a boat, not a bicycle. And I'm always going to take Conker with me in case I lose my cap."

I Love my Puppy

I love my puppy because he wags his tail and comes to meet me.

He barks and jumps in the air when he wants to play, and chases my big bouncy ball.

He fetches a stick for me to throw.

He scampers beside me when we go for walks in the park.

But I love him most when he is sleepy and we snuggle up close.

I Love my Kitten

I love my kitten because she purrs softly when I stroke her.

She pounces on a ball of wool and rolls it between her paws.

She runs along the garden wall and leaps over the gate.

She washes her face by licking her soft padded paws.

She peeps through the cat flap to see if her dinner is ready.

But I love her most of all when she sits with her tail curled all around her.

I Love my Pony

I love my pony because he neighs hello when I come to visit him.

He lets me sponge him and brush his soft shiny mane.

He eats a shiny green apple right out of my hand.

He's fun to be with when we go for long rides.

He jumps at the show and wins a bright red rosette.

But I love him most of all when I talk to him and he nuzzles up close.

I Love my Bunny

I love my bunny because he twitches his nose, and has smooth silky fur.

Bunny nibbles a carrot with his bright white teeth.

He runs in the garden and his fluffy white tail bobs up and down.

He digs a hole in the lawn with his big soft paws.

He sits quietly as I stroke his big floppy ears, and his whiskers twitch up and down.

But I love him most when he dozes off to sleep sitting on my lap.

The Ant and the Grasshopper

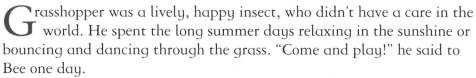

Grasshopper was a lively, happy insect, who didn't have a care in the world. He spent the long summer days relaxing in the sunshine or bouncing and dancing through the grass. "Come and play!" he said to Bee one day.

"I'd love to," said Bee, "but I'm *much* too busy. If I don't gather this pollen, we bees won't be able to make honey. Then, when winter comes, we'll have nothing to eat."

"Well, work if you want to," said Grasshopper. "But *I'd* rather play!" And off he hopped. Then, Grasshopper saw Ladybird crawling along a leaf. "Come and play!" he called.

"Sorry, Grasshopper, not today," replied Ladybird. "I'm looking after the roses. They depend on us to guard them from greenfly!"

"Well, I think you're silly to spend this beautiful day working!" said Grasshopper, hopping away. Grasshopper went happily on his way, until he saw Ant, who was struggling to carry some grain on her back.

"Why are you working so hard?" asked Grasshopper. "It's such a sunny day! Come and play!"

"I have no time, Grasshopper," said Ant. "I have to take this grain back to my nest, so that my family and I have enough food when winter comes. Have you built your nest yet?"

"Nest?" laughed Grasshopper. "Who needs a nest when life in the great outdoors is so wonderful? And there's plenty of food — why should I worry?" And off he hopped.

At night, while the other insects slept, Grasshopper sang and danced under the moonlight. "Come and play!" he called to Spider, who was the only one awake.

"Sorry, Grasshopper," said Spider. "I have a web to spin. Can't stop now!"

"Suit yourself!" said Grasshopper, as he danced away. Day after day, Grasshopper played, while the other insects worked. And, night after night, he danced and sang while the others tried to sleep. The other insects were fed up.

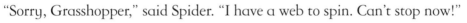

"Stop that noise!" shouted Bee, one night. "You're keeping the whole hive awake!"

"Yes, be quiet!" said Ladybird.

As the summer went on, the long, sunny days began to get shorter and cooler. But lazy Grasshopper hardly noticed. He was still too busy enjoying himself. One day, Grasshopper saw Ant with her seven children. They were all carrying food back to their nest.

"My, look at all your helpers," said Grasshopper.

"Well, we're running out of time," puffed Ant. "What are you doing about building a nest and storing food for the winter?"

"Oh, I can't be bothered," said Grasshopper. "There's lots of food around now, so why worry?"

That night, there was a chill in the air and Grasshopper didn't feel like dancing. "Maybe you'd better start getting ready for winter," warned Spider. It was getting colder, but Grasshopper didn't want to think about that now.

"There's still *loads* of time for that!" said Grasshopper and he began to sing.

Soon the trees began to lose their leaves. Grasshopper was spending more time looking for food, but there wasn't much food to be found. One afternoon, Ant and her children scurried across his path, each carrying a fat, ripe seed. "Where did you find those?" asked Grasshopper, eagerly. "Are there any more?"

"There are plenty over there," said Ant, pointing. "When are you going to make a nest? Winter will be here soon!"

"I'm too hungry to think about that now," said Grasshopper, rushing towards the seeds and gobbling down as many as he could.

A few days later, it began to snow. Ladybird was in her nest, fast asleep. Bee was in her hive, sipping sweet honey with her friends and relations. Grasshopper was cold and all alone. He was hungry and there wasn't a crumb of food to be found anywhere!

THE ANT AND THE GRASSHOPPER

"I know," said Grasshopper. "Ant will help me. She has plenty of food." So he set out to look for Ant's nest. At last, Grasshopper found Ant's cosy nest, safe and warm beneath a rock.

Ant came out to see him. "What do you want?" she asked.

"Please, Ant," said Grasshopper, "have you any food to spare?"

Ant looked at him. "All summer long, while my family and I worked hard to gather food and prepare our nest, what did you do?"

"I played and had fun, of course," said Grasshopper. "That's what summer is for!"

"Well, you were wrong, weren't you," said Ant. "If you play all summer, then you must go hungry all winter."

"Yes," said Grasshopper, sadly, as a tiny tear fell from the corner of his eye. "I have learned my lesson now. I just hope it isn't too late!"

Ant's heart softened. "Okay, come on in," she said. "And I'll find some food for you." Grasshopper gratefully crawled into the warm nest, where Ant and her family shared their food with him.

By the time Spring came around, Grasshopper was fat and fit and ready to start building a nest of his very own!

Billy Bunny's Shopping List

Billy Bunny wanted to play, but Mummy needed his help. "You can tidy the burrow or you can do the shopping," she said. Billy knew that if he went shopping he might see his friends on the way. "I'll do the shopping," he said. Mummy gave him a list. It read: five acorns, two carrots and some parsley.

As Billy went skipping through the woods, a gust of wind blew the list out of his paw and it floated away. "Never mind," said Billy. "I'm sure I'll remember everything!"

But he couldn't remember anything. He met his friend Fox, who said, "Get some flowers. Mummies always like flowers." So Fox and Billy Bunny picked a few bluebells that grew beside the stream.

"What else?" said Billy. "I know – I'll ask Dora Deer. Dora Deer was playing a leaping game near the fallen logs. Billy and Fox joined in, but after a while Billy remembered the shopping.

"If your mummy had written a list, what would be on it?" Billy asked. Dora thought

hard for a minute. "Leaves," she said at
last. "Lots of nice fresh leaves to make
my bed soft. I'm sure leaves were on
your list."

Owl watched them gather a basket
of leaves. "I know what your mummy
wants," she said, blinking wisely. "All
mummies like it when their friends
come to visit. I bet your list said 'Invite
all my friends to tea'."

"Are you sure?" asked Billy. "I think I would have remembered that."
Owl just sniffed and said, "We owls know everything." So Billy ran
around the woods and invited everyone he knew to come to tea
that afternoon.

Billy went home with flowers and leaves. "Don't worry," he told his
mummy. "I lost your list, but I remembered everything – and everyone
is coming to tea this afternoon!" Mummy Bunny didn't have time to be
cross – she had too much to do! Her friend Moose brought some berry
cakes and, by the time everyone arrived for tea, Mummy had almost
forgiven her silly Billy Bunny!

Putting on a Nightgown

Little man in a coal pit
　　Goes knock, knock, knock;
Up he comes, up he comes,
　　Out at the top.

Little Fishes

Little fishes in a brook,
　　Father caught them on a hook,
Mother fried them in a pan,
　　Johnnie eats them like a man.

Ickle Ockle

Ickle, ockle, blue bockle,
　　Fishes in the sea,
If you want a pretty maid,
　　Please choose me.

Jim Crow

Twist about, turn about,
　　Jump Jim Crow;
Every time I wheel about
　　I do just so.

Bob Robin

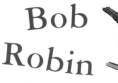

Little Bob Robin,
　　Where do you live?
Up in yonder wood, sir,
　　On a hazel twig.

Old Farmer Giles

Old Farmer Giles,
　　He went seven miles
With his faithful dog Old Rover;
　　And Old Farmer Giles,
When he came to the stiles,
　　Took a run, and jumped clean over.

Fidget

As little Jenny Wren
    Was sitting by the shed,
She waggled with her tail,
    She nodded with her head;
She waggled with her tail,
    She nodded with her head;
As Little Jenny Wren
    Was sitting by the shed.

Praise

Robinets and Jenny Wrens
    Are God Almighty's
        cocks and hens.
The Martins and the Swallows
    Are God Almighty's bows
        and arrows.

In Lincoln Lane

I lost my mare in Lincoln Lane,
    I'll never find her there again;
She lost a shoe,
    And then lost two,
And threw her rider in the drain.

Red Stockings

Red stockings, blue stockings,
    Shoes tied up with silver;
A red rosette upon my breast
    And a gold ring on my finger.

The Dove Says

The dove says, Coo, coo,
    What shall I do?
I can scarce maintain two.
Pooh, pooh, says the wren, I have ten,
And keep them all like gentlemen.
    Curr dhoo, curr dhoo,
Love me, and I'll love you.

Charley Barley

Charley Barley, butter and eggs,
    Sold his wife for three duck eggs.
When the ducks began to lay,
    Charley Barley flew away.

Snow White

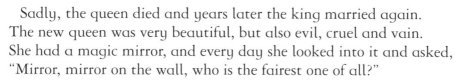

Long, long ago, in a faraway land, there once lived a king and queen who had a beautiful baby girl. Her lips were as red as cherries, her hair as black as coal and her skin as white as snow – her name was Snow White.

Sadly, the queen died and years later the king married again. The new queen was very beautiful, but also evil, cruel and vain. She had a magic mirror, and every day she looked into it and asked, "Mirror, mirror on the wall, who is the fairest one of all?"

And every day, the mirror replied, "You, O Queen, are the fairest!"

Time passed, and every year Snow White grew more beautiful by the hour. The queen became increasingly jealous of her stepdaughter.

One day, the magic mirror gave the queen a different answer to her question. "Snow White is the fairest one of all!" it replied.

The queen was furious and at once invented an evil plan. She ordered her huntsman to take Snow White deep into the forest and kill her.

But the huntsman couldn't bear to harm Snow White. "Run away!" he told her. "Run away and never come back, or the queen will kill us both!" Snow White fled.

As Snow White rushed through the trees she came upon a tiny cottage. She knocked at the door and then went in – the house was empty. There she found a tiny table with seven tiny chairs. Upstairs there were seven little beds. Exhausted, she lay down across them and fell asleep.

Many hours later, Snow White woke to see seven little faces peering at her. The dwarfs, who worked in a diamond mine, had returned home and wanted to know who the pretty young girl was.

Snow White told them her story and why she had to run away. They all sat round and listened to her tale.

When she had finished, the eldest dwarf said, "If you will look after our house for us, we will keep you safe. But please don't let anyone into the cottage while we are at work."

The next morning, when the wicked queen asked the mirror her usual question, she was horrified when it answered, "The fairest is Snow White, gentle and good. She lives in a cottage, deep in the wood!"

The queen turned scarlet with rage; she had been tricked. She magically disguised herself as an old pedlar and set off into the wood to seek out Snow White and kill the girl herself.

That afternoon, Snow White heard a tap-tapping at the window.

She looked out and saw an old woman with a basket full of bright ribbons and laces.

"Pretty things for sale," cackled the old woman.

Snow White remembered the dwarfs' warning. But the ribbons and laces were so lovely, and the old woman seemed so harmless, that she let her in.

"Try this new lace in your dress, my dear," said the old woman. Snow White was thrilled and let the woman thread the laces. But the old woman pulled them so tight that Snow White fainted.

Certain that at last she had killed her stepdaughter, the queen raced through the forest, back to her castle, laughing evilly.

That evening, the dwarfs returned home. They were shocked to discover Snow White lying on the floor – lifeless. They loosened the laces on her dress so she could breathe and made her promise once again not to let in any strangers when they were at work.

The next day, when the mirror told the queen that Snow White was still alive, she was livid and vowed to kill her once and for all. She disguised herself and went back to the cottage.

This time the old woman took with her a basket of lovely red apples. She had poisoned the biggest, reddest one of all. She knocked on the door and called out, "Juicy red apples for sale."

The apples looked so delicious that Snow White just had to buy one. She opened the door and let the old woman in. "My, what pretty, rosy cheeks you have, deary," said the woman, "the very colour of my apples. Here, take a bite and see how good they are." She handed Snow White the biggest one...

Snow White took a large bite and fell to the floor – dead. The old woman fled into the forest, happy at last.

This time, the dwarfs could not bring Snow White back to life. Overcome with grief, they placed her gently in a glass coffin and carried it to a quiet clearing in the forest. And there they sat, keeping watch over their beloved Snow White.

One day, a handsome young prince came riding through the forest and saw the beautiful young girl in the glass coffin. He fell in love with her at once and begged the dwarfs to let him take her back to his castle.

At first the dwarfs refused, but when they saw how much the prince loved their Snow White, they agreed.

As the prince lifted the coffin to carry it away, he stumbled, and the piece of poisoned apple fell from Snow White's mouth, where it had been lodged all this time. Snow White's eyes fluttered open, and she looked up and saw the handsome young man.

"Where am I?" she asked him in a bewildered voice. "And who are you?"

"I am your prince," he said. "And you are safe with me now. Please will you marry me and come to live in my castle?" He leant forward and kissed her cheek.

"Oh, yes, sweet prince," cried Snow White. "Of course I will."

The next day, the magic mirror told the wicked queen of Snow White's good fortune. She flew into a rage and disappeared in a flash of lightning.

Snow White married her prince, and went to live in his castle. The seven dwarfs visited them often, and Snow White and her prince lived happily ever after.

Katy and the Butterfly

As Katy Kitten lay dozing happily in the sun, something tickled her nose. She opened an eye and saw a butterfly hovering above her whiskers, but as she tapped at it with her soft paw it fluttered away. Katy sprang after the butterfly, missed it and landed with a howl in a bed of thistles. "I'll catch that butterfly!" she said, crossly.

Katy chased the butterfly towards the stream, where it settled on the branch of a tree. She climbed after it, high into the tree, but every time she came near, the butterfly simply flew away – and by now, she was stuck! Nervously, she looked down at the stream swirling below her.

Just then, the butterfly fluttered past her nose. Without thinking, Katy swiped at it with her paw. But as she did so, she lost her balance and went tumbling down through the tree, landing with a great SPLASH! in the water below. "Help!" cried Katy, waving her paws wildly.

Luckily she caught hold of a branch hanging over the stream and clambered onto the bank.

Katy arrived home, cold and wet. She curled up, exhausted, in front of the fire, but just as she started to doze, she felt something tugging at her whiskers. She opened one eye and saw a little mouse.

"Oh no, I've done enough chasing for one day, thank you!" said Katy.

Going to Nursery

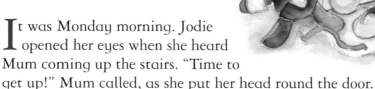

It was Monday morning. Jodie opened her eyes when she heard Mum coming up the stairs. "Time to get up!" Mum called, as she put her head round the door.

"Don't you want to go and see the nursery?"

"Yes, I do!" Jodie said. She wanted to find out more about the nursery that Mum had talked so much about. Jodie jumped out of bed and Mum helped her to get dressed.

"Mum?" said Jodie. "What's it like at nursery?"

"Do you like climbing frames?" Mum asked her.

"Yes, I do!" said Jodie.

"Then you'll like nursery," Mum said. "There are lots of exciting things, like climbing frames, to play on. Come on, let's hurry up and then you can see for yourself."

Dad was waiting for Jodie in the kitchen. "All ready to look at the nursery?" he said.

Jodie ate her cereal and her toast. "I'm ready!" she cried. "Let's go!" When they arrived at the nursery, a lady was waiting to meet them. "You must be Jodie," she said, smiling.

"I'm Mrs Clark. Would you like to see what we do here?"
Jodie nodded.

Mrs Clark opened a door into a big room full of children
having fun. Some of them were playing on a yellow climbing frame.
Some of them were digging in the sand tray, with buckets and spades.
"Mum," said Jodie, "you were right. There are lots of exciting things to
do at nursery."

Soon, it was time to go, but Jodie had so many questions about
nursery. "When do I start?" she asked, on the way home.

"Next week," said Mum.

While she was eating lunch, Jodie said, "How long will I stay there?"

"Just for the morning, to start with," replied Dad.

Watching television with Mum that afternoon, Jodie asked,
"Can I take teddy with me to nursery?"

"Of course," smiled Mum. "I think he'll enjoy it."

Next morning, Jodie and Mum went to the park. As Jodie was
climbing up the slide, she met a small boy, who was standing at the top.

The little boy's mum smiled at Jodie's mum.
"He's starting at nursery next week," she said.

"So am I!" cried Jodie. "What's your
name?" she asked the boy.

"Jack!" he said, whooshing down the
slide. "Do you like nursery?"

"I think so," Jodie told him.

"I'll see you there," said Jack and
he ran off, waving.

The week quickly passed and, at last, the day came for Jodie to start nursery. She was very excited and a little bit scared, all at the same time.

"Where am I going to put my coat?" she asked Mum, as they pushed open the door of the nursery.

"They'll have your very own place ready for you," said Mum.

"Hello again, Jodie," said Mrs Clark. "Can you see the hook for your coat? It's the one with the blue pig. Now, what would you like to do first?"

Jodie noticed a boy, who was working on a big puzzle of a fire engine. It was Jack.

"Hi, Jack," she said. "Can I help?" She picked up a piece of puzzle and fitted it into place.

"I think it's time for me to go," whispered Mum, giving Jodie a hug.

"Okay, Mum," Jodie smiled. "See you later," and she picked up another piece of puzzle.

"Jodie's really good at this, isn't she?" said Mrs Clark to Jack. Jack nodded – it was fun at nursery.

Then, Mrs Clark asked if they would like to help pass round the drinks and apple slices.

"Oh yes, please," said Jodie and Jack, together.

GOING TO NURSERY

"Everyone, come and meet Jack and Jodie," said Mrs Clark. All the girls and boys came over to say "Hello". Then, Mrs Clark asked Jodie and Jack what they would like to do next. Jodie knew exactly what she wanted to do. She tugged Jack over to the dressing-up box.

"Look!" she said, pulling out two hats, "we could be firemen."

Jack pointed to a big red car, standing in the corner. "And that could be our fire engine," he said.

After Jodie and Jack had put out lots of pretend fires, they saw two girls, busy making things at a table. They ran over to join them. There were boxes and cardboard tubes and glue and paint everywhere.

"Let's make a fire engine," said Jodie.

Jodie started to glue two boxes together. She cut some card circles for wheels and Jack helped her stick them on. Then, they painted the whole thing bright red.

Just as they finished, Jodie's mum slipped in through the door. Jodie ran over to her.

"Come and see," she said, dragging Mum over to the modelling table. "We made a fire engine."

"It's lovely!" smiled Mum. "Shall we take it home with us? It's time for lunch now."

Jodie put on her coat and waved to Jack. "Did you have a good time?" asked Mum. "Do you want to come again?"

"Yes, I do!" cried Jodie. "Nursery is great fun."

Aunty and the Flowers

Every year on the farm, the animals had a competition. Everyone liked to join in the fun, and there was a prize for the winner. The prize could be for anything. One year, it was for growing the best purple vegetables. Once it was for having the knobbliest knees. (Gladys the duck won that, of course.)

This year they decided the prize would be for the best display of flowers. But who would choose the winner?

If Nelly the hen were the judge, she would make herself the winner. She always did. Bramble the sheep caught her wool on everything. She pulled the tables and chairs down behind her wherever she went.

Blink the pig covered everything in mud and Rambo the big horse couldn't even get into the tent!

But Aunty the goat wanted the job. She told the others how much she liked flowers. So why not? Aunty had never been a judge before and so she was chosen.

The big day came. Everyone had been busy for days. The tent was full of flowers, colour and light. Perfect!

The judge, Aunty, came in first. She looked very important and was taken to the first display made by Bramble the sheep.

"So I just choose which flowers I like best?" Aunty asked.

AUNTY AND THE FLOWERS

"Yes, we walk along the table, and whichever display you think is best wins the prize. This is Bramble's display. He has spent all morning getting it right," said Blink the pig.

"It's called 'Daisies and Dandelions'," said Bramble proudly. The flowers were white and yellow and looked very pretty in a blue mug. Aunty looked at them carefully. She sniffed them. And then she ate them.

The others were so surprised that they couldn't speak! They just stared as Aunty went to the next one, "Buttercups and Roses". She ate them too!

The goat tilted her head back, half closed her eyes in a very thoughtful sort of way, and compared "Buttercups and Roses" with "Daisies and Dandelions".

Moving along the line, she ate "Cowslips and Honeysuckle". Then she ate "Chrysanthemums and Poppies". Aunty wrinkled up her nose.

"Bit sour, that," she said. She turned at last and saw all the others looking at her with their mouths open. She looked from one to the other, red poppies drooping from the sides of her mouth.

"What?" she said, puzzled. "What!"

Rambo said, "You were supposed to judge how pretty the flowers are!"

"Flowers are pretty as well?" asked Aunty.

Everyone burst out laughing. They had to explain it all to Aunty. She thought the whole idea of just looking at flowers was very odd.

There was no time to pick more flowers and start again. Instead, they gave Bramble the prize... Aunty had decided that Bramble's flowers tasted the best!

At the end, the judge is always given a bunch of flowers as a small, thankyou gift. Aunty was very pleased... She ate it!

There Were Two Birds Sat on a Stone

There were two birds sat on a stone,
  Fa, la, la, la, lal, de;
One flew away, then there was one,
  Fa, la, la, la, lal, de;
The other flew after, and then there was none,
  Fa, la, la, la, lal, de;
And so the poor stone was left all alone,
  Fa, la, la, la, lal, de!

I am a Pretty Little Dutch Girl

I am a pretty little Dutch girl,
  As pretty as I can be.
And all the boys in the
    neighbourhood
  Are crazy over me!

Five Little Ducks

Five little ducks went swimming one day,
  Over the hills and far away,
Mother Duck said, "Quack, quack, quack, quack,"
  But only four little ducks came back.
One little duck went swimming one day,
  Over the hills and far away,
Mother Duck said, "Quack, quack, quack, quack,"
  And all the five little ducks came back.

There Was an Old Crow

There was an old crow
  Sat upon a clod:
There's an end of my song,
  That's odd!

The Wise Old Owl

There was an old owl who lived in an oak;
　The more he heard, the less he spoke.
The less he spoke, the more he heard.
　Why aren't we like that wise old bird!

The Ostrich

Here is the ostrich straight and tall,
　Nodding his head above us all.
Here is the hedgehog prickly and small,
　Rolling himself into a ball.
Here is the spider scuttling around,
　Treading so lightly on the ground.
Here are the birds that fly so high,
　Spreading their wings across the sky.
Here are the children fast asleep,
　And in the night the owls do peep,
"Tuit tuwhoo, tuit tuwhoo!"

Billy Booster

Billy Billy Booster,
　Had a little rooster,
The rooster died
　And Billy cried.
Poor Billy Booster.

Birds of a Feather

Birds of a feather flock together
　And so will pigs and swine;
Rats and mice shall have their choice,
　And so shall I have mine.

Hazel Squirrel Learns a Lesson

Hazel Squirrel had the finest tail of all the animals that lived beside Looking-Glass Pond.

It was fluffier than Dilly Duck's tail... bushier than Harvey Rabbit's tail... and swooshier than everybody's!

Each morning Hazel groomed her tail and admired her reflection in the pond. "I really do have a beautiful tail!" she would say, smiling at herself in the silvery water.

Sometimes Hazel played with her friends, but it usually ended in tears.

"You splashed my lovely tail!" Hazel would shout crossly, when she played leap-frog with Webster. "You're getting my tail dirty, Harvey!" she would moan very grumpily, when they played digging.

Soon, Hazel stopped playing with her friends altogether.

"I'm far too busy brushing my tail!" she said when they came to call. "Come back some other time."

One morning as usual, Hazel was admiring her tail by the pond. Suddenly, she had a funny thought. She couldn't remember the last time she had seen her friends.

Hazel looked at her reflection in the pond. Staring back was a strange face... a cross face... a grumpy face. It was Hazel's face! Hazel couldn't believe her eyes. "No wonder my friends don't visit me any more," she cried. "I've forgotten how to smile!"

The next day Hazel called for her friends. They had such fun playing leap-frog and digging muddy holes that she forgot all about her tail. "From now on," she laughed, "the only time I'll look at my reflection is to practise smiling!"

The Dragon who was Scared of Flying

Once upon a time, in a land far away, there lived a dragon named Dennis. He lived in a cave high up in the mountains. All his friends lived in caves nearby, and his own brothers and sisters lived right next door. Now you would think that Dennis would have been a very happy dragon, surrounded by his friends and family, wouldn't you? Well, I'm sorry to say that Dennis was, in fact, a very unhappy and lonely dragon.

The reason for this was that Dennis was scared of flying. Every day his friends would set off to have adventures, leaving poor Dennis behind on his own. Dennis would stare out of his cave at the departing dragons. How he wished he could join them!

After they had gone, he would stand on the ledge outside his cave, trying to build up the courage to fly. But, as soon as he looked over the edge, he felt all giddy and had to step back. Then he would crawl back into his cave defeated and spend the rest of the day counting the stalactites on the ceiling or rearranging his large collection of bat bones.

Every evening, the other dragons would return with amazing tales of what they had been up to that day. "I rescued a damsel in distress," one would say.

"I fought the wicked one-eyed giant and won," boasted another.

"I helped light the fire for a witch's cauldron," announced a third.

"What have you been up to?" Dennis's sister Doreen used to ask him.

"Oh... um... this and that," Dennis would reply mournfully, looking down at his scaly toes. Then Doreen would lead him out of the cave and try to teach him to fly. Dennis would take a running jump and flap his wings furiously but his feet would stay firmly on the ground. Then the other dragons would laugh so much that, in the end, he always gave up.

One day, Dennis could stand it no longer. The other dragons flew off as usual to find adventure but Dennis, instead of retreating into his cave, set off down the mountain side. It was very tiring having to walk. Dennis had never really been further than from his cave to the ledge and back, and soon he was puffing and panting. He was about to rest at the side of the path when his eye was caught by something colourful in the distance. Down in the valley he could make out some brightly coloured tents, and now he could hear the faint strains of music drifting up to him. "I'd better take a closer look," thought Dennis. "Maybe I can have an adventure, like the other dragons!" He got so excited at the thought of his very own adventure that he started to run.

At last Dennis reached the tents and found himself in a world more exotic than he could ever imagine. He was surrounded by creatures such as he had never seen before. There was a yellow creature that roared and another one with stripes and fierce teeth. There were also quite a few hairy creatures with long tails. Can you guess what all these creatures were? Of course, Dennis had never seen a lion or a tiger or a chimpanzee before. He thought they were very peculiar! The animals thought Dennis was very odd, too. They stood in a circle around him. "How strange," snarled the lion. "A slimy thing with wings!"

"Look at its funny, knobbly tail," giggled the chimpanzees.

Dennis began to feel unhappy and unwanted again, but at that moment he heard a friendly voice saying, "Hello, there! Welcome to Chippy's Circus. I'm Claude the clown. How do you do?"

Dennis turned round. Now he felt really confused, for standing behind him was a man with the unhappiest face Dennis had ever seen. He had great sad eyes and a mouth that was turned down so far that it seemed to touch his chin. Yet he spoke so cheerfully!

"I'm Dennis the dragon," said Dennis.

"A dragon, eh?" said Claude. "Well, we've never had a dragon in the circus before. Might be quite a crowd puller! Would you like to join the circus?" he asked.

"Oh, yes please," cried Dennis.

"Good!" said Claude. "I'm sure you're very talented," he added.

So Dennis joined the circus and was happy for the first time in his life. The other animals became friendly when they knew what he was. Claude taught Dennis to ride the unicycle and to do acrobatic tricks. He also learned how to dive into a bucket of water. He didn't mind that a bit because his slimy skin was quite waterproof!

Now, as you know, dragons are particularly good at breathing fire, so Dennis soon became the circus's champion fire-eater. Folk would come from far and near to see Dennis shooting flames high into the dark roof of the big top.

One evening, when Dennis had finished his fire-eating act, he sat eating an ice cream to cool his hot throat and watched Carlotta, the tight-rope walker. She was pirouetting high up on the rope as usual. Then all at once she lost her footing and Dennis saw to his horror that she was going to fall. He dropped his ice cream and, without thinking, flapped his wings furiously. As Carlotta fell, Dennis found himself flying up towards her. He caught her gently on his back and flew down to the ground with her clinging on tightly. The crowd roared and burst into applause. They obviously thought it was all part of the act.

"Thank you, Dennis," whispered Carlotta in Dennis's ear. "You saved my life."

Dennis was overjoyed. Not only had he saved Carlotta's life, he had also learned to fly. And he said with a grin, "I do declare that flying is actually rather fun."

Home Sweet Home

Bella Bunny looked at the sweet green grass growing in the meadow on the far side of the stream. She was tired of eating the rough grass that grew near her burrow. "I'm going to cross the stream!" she said to her brothers and sisters, pointing to a fallen branch that lay across it.

Bella bounced safely across the branch and was soon eating the sweet, juicy grass on the other side of the stream. Her brothers and sisters thought she was very brave and wondered if they should follow. But just then, they saw a sly fox creeping up behind Bella through the grass!

"Look out!" they called.

Bella turned to see the fox just in time! She leapt back onto the branch, but she was in such a hurry that she slipped and fell into the stream. Luckily, Becky Beaver had been watching and she pulled Bella safely to the other side.

"Home sweet home!" gasped Bella, with relief. And she ran off to join her brothers and sisters, vowing never to leave home again.

Vicky the Very Silly Vet

"Good morning!" calls Vicky Vet as she opens the door to her surgery. "How are all my animals today?"

Vicky starts her early morning rounds with the Goldie Goldfish. Vicky Vet loves looking after animals but sometimes she gets very mixed up! She knows she has a busy morning ahead of her, so Vicky wants to get all the cages cleaned, and the animals fed, before her first patient arrives. "I'll give you some clean newspaper first, Patch," she says to the messy puppy, "and then I'll give your blanket a good shake, Tabby."

"There you are, Tabby. A nice fluffy bed for you," says Vicky, putting the blanket back into Tabby's basket, when... Brriiing, brriiing! Brriiing, brriiing! "That's the phone, Tabby," she cries.

Vicky Vet drops everything and rushes to answer it. "Now, where was I?" thinks Vicky Vet to herself, coming back to the cages.

"I was just about to give you some fresh wood chips, wasn't I?" she says to Hickory and Dickory, the two mice. Just as she is putting the wood chips in the mouse cage...

Ding dong! goes the doorbell. "Who can that be?" Vicky wonders.

"My first patient's not due for half an hour!" Vicky hasn't noticed that the cage doors are open and Patch is busy chasing Tabby around the room!

It is Polly Postlady with a parcel that is too big to fit through the letterbox. "Thank you, Polly," says Vicky, "but I don't think this parcel is for me. It's addressed to Tony's Pizza Parlour."

"Oh dear!" says Polly Postlady. "How could I be so potty? Sorry, Vicky!"

"Now," says Vicky Vet, "I think I was about to clean Percy Parrot's cage." She has just finished cleaning the cage when she feels something scampering up her leg!

"Oh no!" cries Vicky. "Hickory and Dickory, how did you escape? "And Patch and Tabby! How did you get out?" Very silly Vicky is flapping about trying to catch all the animals, and all the time Percy is hopping closer to the open door of his cage. Vicky dives at Tabby and pounces on Hickory and Dickory and is busy chasing Patch back into his cage when… SUDDENLY there is a loud squawk! Percy Parrot is flying towards the open window!

"Wait! Percy! Stop!" she cries, rushing after the parrot. Luckily, Vicky catches Percy just in time. Once he is safely back in his cage, she manages to round up Hickory and Dickory, get Tabby back into her basket, and shut Patch safely into his cage.

"Phew!" she puffs. "I feel as if I've done a whole morning's work already. "I think after all this, it must be time for some breakfast!"

Vicky lines up the feeding bowls and animal feed on the table. Carefully, she measures out some delicious dog food for Patch and gives him a big juicy bone to chew. Then she spoons out some crunchy bird seed for Percy, some fishy cat food for Tabby, and some tasty sunflower seeds for the mice. Vicky has nearly finished making breakfast for the animals when… Ding dong! It's the doorbell again.

"Oh!" she cries. "My first patient is here already! I'd better hurry!" As quickly as she can, Vicky puts the food bowls in the cages – but she doesn't look to see who is getting what! So Patch the dog gets a bowl of crunchy bird seed. Hickory and Dickory the mice get the dog food and the big juicy bone. Tabby the cat gets the tasty sunflower seeds. And Percy the parrot gets the fishy cat food! What's more, Vicky is in such a rush that she leaves all the cage doors open again!

This time, though, the animals know just what to do. Hickory and Dickory find their sunflower seeds in Tabby's basket. Tabby discovers her fishy cat food in Percy's cage. Percy pecks at his bird seed in Patch's cage. And Patch finds his delicious dog food in the mouse cage.

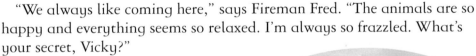

Fred Fireman is at the door with his dog Dot for a check-up.

"Come in," says Vicky Vet. "You're right on time."

"We always like coming here," says Fireman Fred. "The animals are so happy and everything seems so relaxed. I'm always so frazzled. What's your secret, Vicky?"

Very silly Vicky thinks about her crazy morning and wonders what dreadful mess will greet Fred as they walk into the surgery. But clever Patch, Tabby, Percy and the mice are back in their own cages. Vicky sees the clean and tidy room and grins at her animals.

"Treats for tea," she whispers!

Webster
the
Littlest Frog

Webster was the littlest frog on the pond, and he was fed up. Fed up with being bossed about. Fed up with playing on his own. Fed up, in fact, with being the littlest frog. None of the bigger frogs would let Webster play games with them.

"Hop it, Titch!" they croaked. "You're far too small to join in our games."

Every day, Webster sat on his own, watching the other frogs play leap-frog on Looking-Glass Pond.

"You don't have to be a big frog to jump," thought Webster, as he watched. "I can do that."

At last, one bright, moonlit evening Webster found the courage to ask the other frogs if he could join in.

"Please let me play with you," said Webster. "I can jump really high!"

The other frogs just laughed.

"But I can!" he insisted. He took a deep breath. "I can jump... over the moon!"

The other frogs laughed so much, they nearly fell off their lily pads.

"I'll prove it!" he said. "Just watch me."

One... two... three JUMP! Webster leapt off his lily pad and sailed over the moon's reflection in the pond.

The other frogs stared in amazement. It was true. Webster could jump over the moon!

"We're sorry we didn't believe you," said one of the big frogs.

"Of course you can play with us. You might not be the biggest frog on the pond, but you certainly are the cleverest!"

Fishes Swim

Fishes swim in water clear,
  Birds fly up into the air,
Serpents creep along the ground,
  Boys and girls run round and round.

Cut Thistles

Cut thistles in May,
  They'll grow in a day;
Cut them in June,
  That is too soon;
Cut them in July,
  Then they will die.

Little Robin and Pussycat

Little Robin Redbreast jumped
  upon a wall,
Pussycat jumped after him,
  and almost got a fall!
Little Robin chirped and sang,
  and what did pussy say?
Pussycat said, "Mew" and
  Robin jumped away.

Little Robin Redbreast sat upon a tree,
  Up went pussycat, and down
    went he!
Down came pussy, and away Robin ran;
  Says little Robin Redbreast,
    "Catch me if you can!"

Feathers

Cackle, cackle, Mother Goose,
  Have you any feathers loose?
Truly have I, pretty fellow,
  Half enough to fill a pillow.
Here are quills, take one or two,
  And down to make a bed for you.

You Shall be Queen

Lilies are white,
   Rosemary's green,
When I am king,
   You shall be queen.

Jemmy Dawson

Brave news is come to town,
   Brave news is carried;
Brave news is come to town,
   Jemmy Dawson's married.

First he got a porridge-pot,
   Then he bought a ladle;
Then he got a wife and child,
   And then he bought a cradle.

My Little Cow

I had a little cow,
   Hey diddle, ho diddle!
I had a little cow,
   and I drove it to the stall;
hey diddle, ho diddle!
   and there's my song all.

The Coachman

Up at Piccadilly oh!
   The coachman takes his stand,
And when he meets a pretty girl,
   He takes her by the hand;
Whip away for ever oh!
   Drive away so clever oh!
All the way to Bristol oh!
   He drives her four-in-hand.

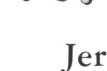

Jerry Hall

Jerry Hall,
   He is so small,
A rat could eat him,
   Hat and all.

Misery the Grumpy Fairy

Misery didn't have any friends. It was her own fault, she was always grumbling. She grumbled at the fairy who baked the bread. She even grumbled at the fairy who collected her honey. Willow, her niece, couldn't understand her. "Why do you always find fault with everyone?" she asked.

"Because everybody is so useless," said her grumpy aunt. One day Misery told the fairy who baked the bread, "Your bread is too soft. I like crusty bread."

"If that's your attitude," said the baker fairy, "you can bake your own bread." "I shall!" said Misery.

The next day she was rude to the fairy who mended her shoes.

"No one speaks to me like that!" said the cobbler fairy. "From now on you can mend your own shoes." "I'll be glad to," said Misery grumpily.

Then she insulted the fairy who collected the honey from the honeybees. "How dare you?" said the fairy. "I'm not staying here to be insulted. You can collect your own honey." And she stormed off. Soon there was no one in the village who would do anything for Misery.

"How are you going to manage?" asked Willow.

"No problem," said Misery. "I shall do everything myself." And with that she set to work to bake some bread. Misery lit the fire to get the oven really hot, then she mixed and kneaded the dough until her arms ached, then she left it to rise. Then she put the loaf in the oven, and sat down for a well-earned rest. But, Misery fell asleep until a smell of burning woke her! All that was left of the loaf of bread were a few burnt cinders. What Misery didn't realise was that the baker fairy used a special baking spell – a spell that Misery didn't know!

Misery was still determined to carry on. She went to collect some honey from the bees. She watched them buzzing round the hive. Misery just waved her arms at them, shouting, "Out of my way, bees." They didn't like it one little bit! Their answer was to swarm around her and sting her nose and chin. You see, what Misery didn't know was that the honey fairy used the special honey-collecting spell.

Misery ran from the bees as fast as she could and, as she did, she lost her shoe! Oh dear! What a state she was in! Burnt bread, bee stings on her nose and chin, and only one shoe!

"You can't go on like this," said Willow, when she saw her. Misery did some serious thinking. "Tell all the fairies I've turned over a new leaf," she told Willow. "From now on I shan't be a grumpy fairy any more."

Willow was delighted! So were the other fairies. Misery didn't complain about anything for months after that, and Willow kept her fingers crossed that it would last!

A Friend
for
Barney

It was Saturday morning at Faraway Farm. Danny, Rosie and Conker the dog went down to the pond to feed some breadcrumbs to the ducks. "All the ducks are friends," said Rosie. "They never fight about who gets the biggest piece."

"Not like you," said Danny.

"That's because you always get the biggest piece," said Rosie.

When they went to see the chickens, Danny asked, "Are they friends too?"

"I think so," said Rosie, "but some of them are a bit pecky."

"What about the pigs? Sometimes Bessie can be a bit grumpy with her piglets," said Danny.

"Oh, that's just because she is their mum," said Rosie, "and they are very greedy sometimes so Bessie has to tell them off. She is very friendly really."

"Everybody at Faraway Farm has friends," agreed Danny. "Even the red tractor is friends with the old blue van."

"My best friend is Stan," said Rosie.

"Cats are boring," declared Danny. "They just sleep all the time. My best friend is Conker. He is the fastest dog in the world and he can catch sticks in the air. Watch this!"

"But Barney the scarecrow doesn't have a friend," said Rosie frowning. "He just stands on the hill all day with no one to talk to. Let's go and see him."

When they went back to the house, Rosie said to her mum, "Barney's lonely. I want him to have a friend."

"Then why don't you make him one?" asked Mum.

In the afternoon Mum took them to a jumble sale in town so they could get some clothes for a new scarecrow.

Danny found an old pair of sports shoes and a pair of motorbike gloves. Rosie found a nice pink party dress and a hat with a green ribbon. They asked Dad if he would help them to make a scarecrow. "Yes," said Dad. "All we need is a sack and some straw and a big pumpkin."

Danny stuffed the sack with straw and Dad helped Rosie to paint a face on the pumpkin. "She looks friendly already," smiled Rosie.

"But she'll still scare the birds," said Danny. Mum made some hair out of wool, then she found a necklace and a bright blue handbag.

"What a beauty," said Dad. "All she needs is a name."

"I want to call her Mary, like my favourite dolly," said Rosie.

"Scary Mary Crow," said Danny. "That's a great name." So, that's what they called her. They took Scary Mary up the hill.

"Hello, Barney," greeted Danny. "We've brought you a friend."

"Now you won't be lonely any more," added Rosie.

"I think Barney likes her," said Danny.

"He can see by looking at the boots she is wearing that she's very good at football."

"I think he likes her because she has a smiley face," said Rosie. Dad put some money in Barney's pocket and some more in Mary's handbag. "Now they can go to the beach and buy an ice cream," he said.

Rosie skipped all the way home to tell Stan the cat all about Scary Mary. "I'm very happy, Stan," she said, giving him a big hug. "Now everybody at Faraway Farm has got a friend."

The Night Carnival

Jim was a boy who hated the night, it made him feel lonely and gave him a fright. One night a bright light seemed to be coming from outside, so he pulled back the curtains – and gasped in surprise...

There was a bright, shiny lantern outside his window! "It's carnival time!" cried the lantern, grinning. "There's an adventure for everyone, why don't you join in?"

"I'm on my way!" cried young Jim, and with a skip and a jump, he slid down the drainpipe. Jim joined in the fun, dancing all night. But when it was time to go back to his room, Jim looked sad.

"Whatever is the matter?" asked the lantern.

"My room is full of monsters, and I'm scared of the dark," replied Jim.

"They aren't monsters at all," the lantern replied. "They are carnival folk – so there's no need to hide!"

The lantern and his friends left, and the room grew dark, but when Jim looked out from behind his hands he didn't see monsters, he saw carnival bands!

The Queen of the Monsters

Towards the end of every year all the monsters meet in a huge cave to vote for their new queen. The tales of their misbehaviour make the headlines in the newspapers every year but, this time Mog decided she would see for herself.

As she arrived, Mog heard Trundle the Troll let out one of his infamous roars in the depths of the cave. The sound was so loud that it knocked her over! As she picked herself up Hagar the Hairy, who was terribly scary, strode past. The huge claws on the ends of his paws scratched the ground, and he left a trail of digusting dribble.

Slod the Slimeball was the favourite to win – she was a disgrace, even for a monster! But the monsters all crowded round little Mog. They were fascinated by her, she was so small and sweet. She had four dainty feet and a charming smile – not very monstrous at all!

After they had voted, the monsters sat down for a banquet. The noise was appalling as they discussed who should win and Mog felt sure that Slod the Slimeball would be the new queen.

But when the decision was announced, Mog was amazed to hear that she was to be the new queen! For once the monsters had decided that they didn't want a queen they would dread – so they voted for little Mog instead!

Nibbling Neighbours

One sunny morning in the meadow, Annabel was happily munching away when she was surprised to discover a hole where there should be grass. "My dears," she mooed, "there's a hole in our field!"

There was no doubt about it. Someone had dug a round, deep hole in the ground.

"We must be careful not to fall into it," said Poppy, anxiously.

But the next morning, where there had been one hole before, now there were five! "If this goes on," said Poppy, "we'll have nowhere to stand at all!"

"And nothing to eat," added Emily, sounding alarmed.

By the end of the week,

there were over a hundred holes all over the meadow.

"You've got some nibbling neighbours," said Old MacDonald. "It looks like a family of rabbits has come to stay."

The cows shuddered. "Those hopping things with long ears?" asked Heather. "I can't look my best with them around!"

"And they have very, very large families," warned Emily. "Not just one baby at a time, like cows do."

"It's odd we've never seen one," said Poppy thoughtfully. "Maybe they do their digging in the dark. I'm going to keep watch tonight."

That night, as the full moon rose over the meadow, Poppy pretended to go to sleep.

Although she was expecting it, she was shocked when two bright little eyes and a twitchy nose popped up right in front of her.

"Aaaaaghh!" cried Poppy.

"Aaaaaghh!" cried the rabbit, and disappeared down its hole as fast as it had come.

"You should have followed it!"

cried Annabel, who had been woken by the sudden noises.

"Down a rabbit hole?" gasped Emily. "Don't be silly, Annabel. She's far too big!"

"Then we're doomed," said Heather, gloomily. "Those rabbits will take over without us even seeing them do it."

The next morning, the cows awoke to an amazing sight. Hundreds of rabbits were sitting all around them.

"Excuse me!" said the largest one. "We have come to ask for your help."

"Help?" echoed Annabel. "We're the ones who need help!"

The rabbit explained that his family lived in fear. "Your hooves are so big, you could stamp on us without noticing."

Just then, Poppy had one of her excellent ideas. "You would be much safer," she said, "if you lived under the hedgerow."

And they did. All day in the meadow, there's munching, mooing and mumbling. All night in the hedgerow, there's nibbling, digging and wiggling. And everyone is happy.

The Enchanted Garden

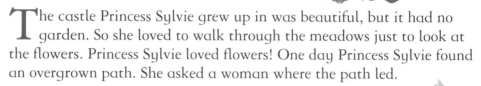

The castle Princess Sylvie grew up in was beautiful, but it had no garden. So she loved to walk through the meadows just to look at the flowers. Princess Sylvie loved flowers! One day Princess Sylvie found an overgrown path. She asked a woman where the path led.

"To the garden of the enchantress!" said the woman.

"What is an enchantress?" Princess Sylvie asked.

"Someone who uses magic! So be warned… don't pick the flowers or who knows what terrible things might happen!"

Princess Sylvie followed the path until she came to a small cottage with the prettiest garden she had ever seen! It was filled with flowers of every colour and perfume!

After that, Princess Sylvie went every day. Winter came and snow lay thick, yet the garden stayed the same. Princess Sylvie forgot all about the enchantress. One wintry day, she picked a rose from the garden and took it back to the castle. As she put it in water, Princess Sylvie suddenly remembered the warning! She'd picked a flower from the enchanted garden and who knew what terrible things might happen?

But days passed and nothing happened. The rose stayed as fresh as the day it was picked. Then months passed and still

nothing happened. Forgetting her fears, Princess Sylvie went back to the enchanted garden.

When she saw the garden, Princess Sylvie wanted to cry! The grass was brown. The flowers had withered and died! Then she heard someone weeping. Inside the cottage the enchantress was sitting by the fire, crying. She was old and bent. Princess Sylvie was afraid, but she felt sorry for her.

"What happened to your lovely garden?" Princess Sylvie asked.

"Someone picked a rose from my magic garden!" said the enchantress. "The picked flower will live forever, but the rest must die! When the rose was picked, my magic was lost! And now, I too will wither and die!"

"What can I do?" said Princess Sylvie, heartbroken.

"Only a princess can bring my magic back," she replied. "She must bring me six sacks of stinging nettles! No princess would do that!"

Princess Sylvie ran to the meadow. She gathered up six sacks of nettles, not caring that they stung her. She took them back to the enchantress.

The enchantress said, "But the nettles must be picked by a princess."

"I *am* a princess," said Princess Sylvie.

Without delay, the enchantress made a magic potion with the nettles and drank it. Instantly, the garden became enchanted again! Princess Sylvie gasped! Gone was the bent old lady and in her place was a beautiful young woman.

"My beautiful garden is restored," smiled the enchantress, "and so am I!"

And so the enchantress and the princess became great friends and shared the enchanted garden.

Oranges and Lemons

Oranges and lemons,
  Say the bells of St Clements.
I owe you five farthings,
  Say the bells of St Martins.
When will you pay me?
  Say the bells of Old Bailey.
When I grow rich,
  Say the bells of Shoreditch.

London Bridge is Falling Down

London bridge is falling down,
  Falling down, falling down,
London bridge is falling down,
  My fair lady.

Frère Jacques

Frère Jacques, Frère Jacques,
  Dormez-vous, dormez-vous?
Sonnez les matines,
  Sonnez les matines,
Ding, dang, dong,
  Ding, dang, dong.

The Miller of Dee

There was a jolly miller
  Lived on the river Dee:
He worked and sang from morn till night,
  No lark so blithe as he;
And this the burden of his song
  For ever used to be –
I jump mejerrime jee!
  I care for nobody – no! not I,
Since nobody cares for me.

Ding Dong Bell

Ding, dong, bell,
　Pussy's in the well!
Who put her in?
　Little Tommy Green.
Who pulled her out?
　Little Johnny Stout.
What a naughty boy was that
　To try to drown poor pussycat,
Who never did any harm,
　But killed the mice in his
　　father's barn.

The Bells of London

Gay go up and gay go down,
　To ring the bells of London town.
Halfpence and farthings,
　Say the bells of St Martin's.
Pancakes and fritters,
　Say the bells of St Peter's.
Two sticks and an apple,
　Say the bells of Whitechapel.

Little Cottage in the Wood

Little cottage in the wood,
　Little old man by the window stood,
Saw a rabbit running by,
　Knocking at the door.
"Help me! Help me! Help me!" he said,
　"Before the huntsman shoots me dead."
"Come little rabbit, come inside,
　Safe with me abide."

Have You Seen the Muffin Man?

Have you seen the muffin man,
　the muffin man, the muffin man,
Have you seen the muffin man
　that lives in Drury Lane O?

Yes, I've seen the muffin man,
　the muffin man, the muffin man;
Yes, I've seen the muffin man who
　lives in Drury Lane O.

Goldilocks and the Three Bears

Once upon a time, deep in a dark green forest, there lived a family of bears. There was great big Daddy Bear. There was middle-sized Mummy Bear. And there was little Baby Bear.

One sunny morning, the bears were up early, hungry for their breakfast. Daddy Bear cooked three bowls of porridge. He made it with lots of golden, runny honey, just the way bears like it. "Breakfast is ready!" called Daddy Bear.

But, when he poured it into the bowls, it was far too hot to eat!

"We'll just have to let our porridge cool down for a while before we eat it," said Mummy Bear.

"But I'm hungry!" wailed Baby Bear.

"I know, let's go for a walk in the forest while we wait," suggested Mummy Bear. "Get the basket, Baby Bear. We can gather some wild berries as we go."

So, leaving the steaming bowls of porridge on the table, the three bears went out into the forest. The last one out was little Baby Bear, and he forgot to close the front door behind him.

The sun was shining brightly through the trees that morning and someone else was walking in the forest. It was a little girl called Goldilocks, who had long, curly golden hair and the cutest nose you ever did see.

Goldilocks was skipping happily through the forest when suddenly she smelt something yummy and delicious – whatever could it be?

She followed the smell until she came to the three bears' cottage. It seemed to be coming from inside. The door was open, so she peeped in and saw three bowls of porridge on the table.

Goldilocks just couldn't resist the lovely, sweet smell. So, even though she knew she wasn't ever supposed to go into anyone's house without first being invited, she tiptoed inside.

First, she tasted the porridge in Daddy Bear's great big bowl. "Ouch!" she said. "This porridge is *far* too hot!" So she tried the porridge in Mummy Bear's middle-sized bowl. "Yuck!" said Goldilocks. "This porridge is *far* too sweet!" Finally, she tried the porridge in Baby Bear's tiny little bowl. "Yummy!" she said, licking her lips. "This porridge is *just right*!" So Goldilocks ate it *all* up – every last drop!

Goldilocks was so full up after eating Baby Bear's porridge that she decided she must sit down. First, she tried sitting in Daddy Bear's great

big chair. "Oh, dear!" she said. "This chair is *far* too hard!" So she tried Mummy Bear's middle-sized chair. "Oh, no!" said Goldilocks. "This chair is *far* too soft!" Finally, she tried Baby Bear's tiny little chair. "Hurray!" she cried. "This chair is *just right*!" So she stretched out and made herself very comfortable.

But Baby Bear's chair wasn't *just right*! It was *far* too small and, as Goldilocks settled down, it broke into lots of little pieces!

Goldilocks picked herself up off the floor and brushed down her dress. Trying out all of those chairs had made her *very* tired. She looked around the cottage for a place to lie down and soon found the three bears' bedroom.

First, Goldilocks tried Daddy Bear's great big bed. "Oh no, this won't do!" she said. "This bed is *far* too hard!" So she tried Mummy Bear's middle-sized bed. "Oh, bother!" said Goldilocks. "This bed is *far* too soft!" Finally, she tried

Baby Bear's tiny little bed. "Yippee!" she cried. "This bed is *just right*!" So Goldilocks climbed in, pulled the blanket up to her chin and fell fast, fast asleep.

Not long after, the three bears came home from their walk, ready for their yummy porridge. But, as soon as they entered their little cottage, they knew something wasn't quite right.

"Someone's been eating my porridge!" said Daddy Bear, when he looked at his great big bowl.

"Someone's been eating my porridge!" said Mummy Bear, looking at her middle-sized bowl.

"Someone's been eating *my* porridge," cried Baby Bear, looking sadly at his tiny little bowl. "And they've eaten it *all up*!"

Then Daddy Bear noticed that his chair had been moved. "Look, Mummy Bear! Someone's been sitting in my chair!" he said in his deep, gruff voice.

"Look, Daddy Bear! Someone's been sitting in my chair," said Mummy Bear, as she straightened out the cushions on it.

"Someone's been sitting in *my* chair, too," cried Baby Bear. "And look! They've broken it all to pieces!" They all stared at the bits of broken chair. Then Baby Bear burst into tears.

Suddenly, the three bears heard the tiniest of noises. Was it a creak? Was it a groan? Where was it coming from? No, it was a snore, and much to their surprise, it was coming from their bedroom. They crept up the stairs very, very slowly and quietly, to see what was making the noise…

"Someone's been sleeping in my bed!" cried Daddy Bear.

"Someone's been sleeping in my bed," said Mummy Bear.

"Someone's been sleeping in *my* bed!" cried Baby Bear. "And she's still there!"

All this noise woke Goldilocks up with a start.

When she saw the three bears standing over her, Goldilocks was very scared. "Oh, dear! Oh, dear! Oh, dear!" she cried, jumping out of Baby Bear's bed. She ran out of the bedroom, down the stairs, out of the front door and all the way back home — and she never ever came back to the forest again!

The Clumsy Fairy

Did you know that all fairies have to go to school to learn how to be fairies? They have to learn how to fly, how to be graceful and how to do magic. Clementine found it difficult! Poor Clementine. She was the worst in the class. She was clumsy and awkward. When they were dancing she was the only fairy who tripped over her own feet.

"Clementine! Think of feathers, not elephants," Madam Bouquet, the fairy dance teacher, was forever saying. At the end of term all the fairies were given a special task for the holidays. But there was one task that no one wanted. This was to help a little girl who had measles.

"Clementine," said Madam Bouquet, "I want you to paint this rose petal lotion on the little girl's spots every night when she is asleep," said Madam Bouquet. "If you do this for one week, the spots will disappear."

That night Clementine flew in through the little girl's window. So far so good! The little girl's name was Alice, and Clementine could see her fast asleep in bed. She was holding a fat, round teddy in her arms.

Clementine crept towards the bed. Then a toy clown, with a silly face, pinched her bottom! "Ouch!" she yelled.

Alice woke up. "Who's there?" she asked sleepily.

"It's Clementine," said the fairy. "Your clown pinched my bottom!"

Then Clementine overbalanced and sat down quickly on Alice's hot water bottle which was lying on the floor. It was so bouncy she shot straight up in the air and landed with a plop on Alice's bed.

"Are you all right?" asked Alice, rubbing her eyes again, to make sure she wasn't seeing things.

Clementine explained to Alice why she had come. "I'm sorry I woke you," she added. "You're not really supposed to see me."

Alice didn't mind. It was lovely to be able to talk to a real fairy. "Can you really do magic?" she asked Clementine.

"Yes," Clementine told her. "I'm quite good at magic. I just wish I wasn't so clumsy." She told Alice about her dance classes and Alice told Clementine about her ballet lessons.

"If you are helping me get rid of my measles," she said to Clementine, "I'll help you with your ballet." Each night Alice taught Clementine how to point her toes, keep her balance on one foot and curtsy gracefully. But it was the pirouette that Clementine did best of all. Holding her arms high above her head she twirled and twirled round Alice's bedroom.

Each day Clementine painted Alice's spots and by the end of the week they had gone.

After the holidays the fairies went back to school. And, do you know, Clementine was the best dancer in the class. Madam Bouquet couldn't believe her eyes.

"Why, Clementine," she gasped, "you're my prima ballerina!" And "prima", as I'm sure you know, means "first and best"!

Clementine was the happiest fairy in the world!

Such a Pickle!

Old MacDonald has quite a few pigs on his farm. He has two that are favourites – Percy, and the eldest one, Jonathan Jakes Jermington Jollop.

Jonathan Jakes Jermington Jollop is the pig's birth name, but now he is called something much less grand! This is the story of how he got his new name.

When Jonathan Jakes Jermington Jollop was a piglet, he somehow got the idea that he was much better than all the other animals that lived on the farm. It was partly because he had such a long name, and partly because Old MacDonald liked to come and chat to him.

"I don't know what's the matter with that young pig," clucked Henrietta the hen. "I said hello to him this morning, and he didn't say a word. He just put his nose in the air and trotted off."

"He did the very same to me," neighed Old George the horse.

Soon there wasn't an animal left on the farm who had a good word to say about Jonathan Jakes Jermington Jollop – and the piglet only had himself to blame!

So, when Jonathan Jakes Jermington Jollop saw Henry the cockerel standing on the hen house roof, and he decided to climb on to the roof of his sty, that is why no one tried to stop him.

Now, pigs are not well-known for their climbing skills, but this didn't stop Jonathan Jakes Jermington Jollop! He scrabbled and scrambled, puffed and panted, and eventually the young pig found himself perched rather uncomfortably on the top of his sty.

He soon realised that he had a very big problem. Getting up had not been easy, but he could see that getting down was going to be practically impossible – and he discovered that he was scared of heights!

Before long, there was a crowd around the pigsty. There was mooing and baaing, neighing and clucking, as they looked at the panicking pig on the roof.

"How did that silly piglet get into such a pickle?" Annabel the cow mooed.

"What a ridiculous place for a piglet to sit," clucked Henrietta the hen. "That's a place for hens not piglets!"

"Hey, Pickle Piglet!" quacked Doris the duck. "What are you doing up there, and how are you going to get down?" she asked.

"I've been really silly," said Jonathan Jakes Jermington Jollop, looking very upset. "Please help me!"

With a laugh, Old George picked him up by his tail and plonked him on the floor.

Jonathan Jakes Jermington Jollop looked very relieved to have all four trotters on firm ground again, and he smiled happily at the other farm animals as they crowded round him.

Jonathan Jakes Jermington Jollop never put on airs and graces again, and no one let him forget his climbing adventure. From that day on, Jonathan Jakes Jermington Jollop was forever known as Pickles the pig!

Jade
and the
Jewels

Jade was the prettiest mermaid in the lagoon! Her jet black hair reached right down to the tip of her swishy, fishy tail. Her eyes were as green as emeralds, and her skin was as white as the whitest pearl. But Jade was so big-headed and vain that the other mermaids didn't like her!

"That Jade thinks too much of herself!" the other mermaids would say. "One of these days she'll come unstuck!"

But one creature was fond of Jade. Gentle the giant turtle followed her wherever she went. But Jade didn't notice Gentle. She lived in her own world, spending all her time combing her hair and looking in the mirror.

One day Jade overheard the mermaids talking about a pirate ship that had sunk to the bottom of the ocean. On board was a treasure chest filled with precious jewels. "But no one dares take the jewels," whispered the mermaids, "because the pirate ship is cursed!"

"I'm going to find that pirate ship," Jade told Gentle, "and the treasure chest! Just imagine how beautiful I will look wearing all those jewels!" And Jade set off right away.

"Wait for me," called Gentle, paddling after her. "It's too dangerous to go alone!" Jade swam to a deep part of the ocean she had never been to before. She dived through shoals of colourful fish, past the coral reef and deep, deep down to the very bottom of the ocean. Finally, they found the shipwreck.

"Be careful, Jade," said Gentle. "Remember there is a curse on this pirate wreck."

"Nonsense," Jade told him. "I've come to get the jewels and I won't go home without them!" Jade saw the treasure chest through a porthole. Jade swam inside and reached out to touch the chest. The lid sprang open and brilliant jewels spilled over the sides. The colours were dazzling.

Jade lifted out a necklace and put it round her neck. There was a little gold and silver mirror in the chest. She held it up to admire her reflection. The necklace was beautiful! Jade looked lovelier than ever.

Suddenly, there was a loud crack, and the mirror shattered. The necklace turned to stone – it was the ship's curse! Jade tried to swim, but the necklace was so heavy she couldn't move.

"Help!" Jade cried out. "Help! Help!" Gentle the giant turtle heard her and swam to the porthole. "Help me, Gentle," she cried. "Please help me!"

Gentle's powerful flippers broke the necklace and freed Jade. As Jade and Gentle swam away from the wreck, Gentle said, "You don't need fancy jewels, Jade. You're pretty without them."

Once she was safely home, Jade told the other mermaids about the pirate ship curse.

"I've certainly learned my lesson," said Jade. "I'll never be vain again."

Here is the Church

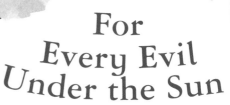

Here is the church,
   Here is the steeple,
Open the doors,
   And here are the people.
Here is the parson, going upstairs,
   And here he is a-saying his prayers.

For Every Evil Under the Sun

For every evil under the sun,
   There is a remedy, or there is none.
If there be one, try and find it;
   If there be none, never mind it.

Matthew, Mark, Luke and John

Matthew, Mark, Luke and John
   Bless the bed that I lie on.
Before I lay me down to sleep,
   I pray the Lord my soul to keep.

Four corners to my bed,
   Four angels there are spread;
Two at the foot, two at the head:
   Four to carry me when I'm dead.

I go by sea, I go by land:
   The Lord made me with His right hand.
Should any danger come to me,
   Sweet Jesus Christ deliver me.

He's the branch and I'm the flower,
   Pray God send me a happy hour;
And should I die before I wake,
   I pray the Lord my soul to take.

I See the Moon

I see the moon,
   And the moon sees me;
God bless the moon,
   And God bless me.

The Key of the Kingdom

This is the key of the kingdom:
    In that kingdom is a city,
In that city is a town,
    In that town there is a street,
In that street there winds a lane,
    In that lane there is a yard,
In that yard there is a house,
    In that house there waits a room,
In that room there is a bed,
    On that bed there is a basket,
A basket of flowers.

Flowers in the basket,
    Basket on the bed,
Bed in the chamber,
    Chamber in the house,
House in the weedy yard,
    Yard in the winding lane,
Lane in the broad street,
    Street in the high town,
Town in the city,
    City in the kingdom:
This is the key of the kingdom.
    Of the kingdom this is the key.

Star Light, Star Bright

Star light, star bright,
    First star I see tonight,
I wish I may, I wish I might,
    Have the wish I wish tonight.

How Many Miles to Babylon?

How many miles to Babylon? –
    Threescore and ten.
Can I get there by candlelight? –
    Aye, and back again!

Twinkle, Twinkle Little Star

Twinkle, twinkle, little star,
    How I wonder what you are!
Up above the world so high,
    Like a diamond in the sky.

O Lady Moon

O Lady Moon, your horns point toward the east:
    Shine, be increased.
O Lady Moon, your horns point toward the west:
    Wane, be at rest.

Elephant

Here is Baby Elephant. Baby Elephant plays with his friends, and he helps them, too.

"Giraffe, you've lost your patterns in the mud," said Baby Elephant. "I'll spray you with my trunk."

"Lion, you look too hot," said Baby Elephant. "I'll shade you with my big ears."

"Monkey, you look very tired," said Baby Elephant. "I'll carry you on my back."

"Oh no, Rhino! You've fallen in the river," said Baby Elephant. "Hold on to my tail very tightly, and I will pull you out."

After his hard work helping his friends, Baby Elephant decided to have a rest under a tree.

"We'll all stay close to Baby Elephant," said his friends, "to make sure he is safe while he rests."

Tiger

Baby Tiger lived in the jungle. One day he fell fast asleep, and his friends could not find him.

"Where is Baby Tiger?" they asked.

Monkey climbed to the top of the highest tree. Rhino ran fast along the riverbank. Elephant searched deep in the jungle.

"Where are you, Baby Tiger?" they called, as loudly as they could.

Then Elephant gave such a loud trumpet that Baby Tiger was woken up.

"Here I am," called Baby Tiger, and with a sleepy yawn and a stretch he waved a stripy paw.

"Baby Tiger! We've been looking everywhere for you," said the animals.

"We couldn't see you because of your stripes," said Monkey.

"We missed you, Baby Tiger," they said, giving him a great big hug.

The  Haughty Princess

There was once a king who had a very
beautiful daughter and many dukes, earls, princes and even kings
came to ask for her hand in marriage. But the princess was proud and
haughty and would have none of them. She would find fault with each
suitor, and send him off with a rude remark.

She said to a plump suitor, "I shall not marry you, Beer Belly."
To a pale faced suitor she said, "I shall not marry you, Death-Mask."
And to a third suitor who was tall and thin she said, "I shall not
marry you, Ramrod." A prince with a red complexion was told,

"I shall not marry you, Beetroot." And so it went on, until every unmarried duke, earl, prince, and even king, had been rejected, and her father thought she would never find a man she liked.

Then a prince arrived who was so handsome and polite, that she found it hard to find a fault with him. But the princess's pride won, and she looked at the curling hairs under his chin and said, a little reluctantly, "I shall not marry you, Whiskers."

The poor king finally lost his temper, "I'm sick of your rudeness. I shall give you to the first beggar who calls at our door for alms, and good riddance to you!"

It wasn't long before a poor beggar knocked at the door, asking for food and clothes. His own clothes were in tatters, his hair dirty, and his beard long and straggling. Sure enough, the king kept his word and he married his daughter to the bearded beggar. The princess cried and and tried to run away, but there was nothing for it.

The beggar led his bride into a wood. He told her that the wood and the land around belonged to the king she had called Whiskers. The princess was even sadder that she had rejected the handsome king, and hung her head in shame when she saw the poor, tumble-down shack where the beggar lived. The place was dirty and untidy, and there was not even a fire burning in the grate. The princess put on a plain dress, helped her husband make the fire, clean the place and prepare a meal.

The beggar gathered some twigs of willow, and after their meal, the two sat together making baskets. But the twigs bruised the princess's fingers, and she cried out with the pain. The beggar was not a cruel man, so he gave her some cloth and thread, and set her to sewing. But although the princess tried hard, the needle made her fingers bleed, and again tears came to her eyes. So the beggar bought a basket of cheap earthenware pots and sent her to market to sell them.

The princess did well at market on the first day, and made a profit. But the next morning, a drunken huntsman rode through the market place, and his mount kicked its way through all the princess's pots. She went home in tears.

The beggar persuaded the cook at the palace of King Whiskers to give his wife a job as a kitchen maid. The princess worked hard, and the cook gave her food to take home. The princess liked the cook, and got on quite well in the kitchen, but she was still sorry she had rejected King Whiskers.

A while later, the palace suddenly got busier, King Whiskers was getting married. "Who is going to marry the king?" asked the princess. But no one knew who the bride was going to be. The princess and the cook decided to go and see what was going on in the great hall. They opened the door quietly and peeped in.

King Whiskers was in the room. He strode over when he saw them. "Spying on the king? You must pay for your nosiness by dancing a jig with me."

The king took her hand, led her into the room, and all the musicians began to play.

But as they whirled around, food began to fly out of her pockets, and everyone in the room roared with laughter. The princess began to run to the door, but the king caught her and took her to one side.

"Do you not realise who I am?" he asked her, smiling kindly. "I am King Whiskers, and your husband the beggar, and the drunken huntsman who broke your pots in the market place. Your father knew who I was, and we arranged all this to rid you of your pride."

The princess was so confused she did not know what to say. All sorts of emotions welled up inside her, but the strongest of all these feelings was love for her husband, King Whiskers.

The palace maids helped her to put on a fine dress fit for a queen. She went back to her husband, and none of the guests realised that the new queen was the poor kitchen maid who had danced a jig with the king.

Baby Bear Finds a Friend

Baby Bear stretched as he woke from his long winter sleep. He took a deep breath of fresh spring air and smiled at the warm sun on his back. He was bursting with energy. Now he needed someone to play with.

"Come and play with me," he called to Owl.

"I only play at night!" said Owl, sleepily.

Nearby some little bunnies were playing. Baby Bear bounded over to join the fun, but Mrs Rabbit shooed him off. "Your paws will hurt my babies," she said. "You can't play with them."

Baby Bear wandered down to the river, where some beavers were hard at work building a dam. "Come and play with me," called Baby Bear.

But the beavers were too busy. So he sat watching Kingfisher diving into the water.

"That looks like fun!" he said, jumping in with a splash!

"Go away!" said Kingfisher. "You will disturb the fish!"

By now Baby Bear was feeling fed up and tired. He lay down in a
hollow and closed his eyes. Then, just as he was drifting to sleep, a voice
said, "Will you come and play with me?" He opened his eyes to see
another bear cub. Baby Bear smiled. "I'm too tired to play now," he
said. "But I'll play with you tomorrow!" And from then on, he was
never lonely again.

Town Mouse and Country Mouse

Once there was a roly-poly, wiggly-whiskered mouse, who lived in a snug little nest under an oak tree. Country Mouse loved his home. He had plenty of acorns, nuts and berries to eat and a warm and cosy straw bed to sleep in. Squirrel and Robin, who lived in the oak tree, were the best neighbours he could ever wish for.

One day, Country Mouse had a surprise. His cousin, Town Mouse, came to visit from the Big City. Town Mouse was sleek and slender, with a smooth, shiny coat. His whiskers were smart and elegant. Country Mouse felt a little ordinary beside him. But he didn't mind. All he wanted to do was make Town Mouse feel welcome. "Are you hungry, Cousin?" he said. "Come and have some supper!"

But Town Mouse didn't like the acorns and blackberries that Country Mouse gave him to eat. They were tough and sour. And Town Mouse thought his cousin's friends were boring. The straw bed that he slept in that night was so rough and scratchy that he didn't sleep a wink!

Next day, Town Mouse said, "Come to the Big City with me, Cousin. It's so much more exciting than the country! I live in a grand house, eat delicious food and have exciting adventures. Come with me and see what you've been missing!" It sounded so wonderful, Country Mouse couldn't resist it. Saying goodbye to his friends, the cousins set off for the city.

When they arrived in the Big City, Country Mouse was frightened. It was so noisy — horns blared and wheels clattered all around them. Huge lorries roared and rumbled down the street and the smelly, smoky air made them choke and cough. And there were dogs *everywhere*!

At last, they arrived safely at Town Mouse's house. It was very grand, just as Town Mouse had said. But it was *so* big! Country Mouse was afraid that he would get lost!

"Don't worry," said Town Mouse to Country Mouse. "You'll soon learn your way around the house. For now, just stay close to me. I'm starving — let's go and have a snack." Country Mouse was hungry, too, so he followed his cousin to the kitchen.

Country Mouse had never seen so much delicious food — there were plates full of fruit, nuts, cheese and cakes.

He and his cousin ate and ate and ate! But Country Mouse wasn't used to this sort of rich food. Before he knew it, his tummy was aching.

Suddenly, a huge woman came into the room. "Eek! Mice!" she screamed. She grabbed a big broom and began to swat the mice, who scampered off as fast as they could.

As the two mice scurried across the floor, Country Mouse thought things couldn't possibly get worse. But how wrong he was! A big cat suddenly sprang out from behind a chair! With a loud "MEEOOWW," he pounced on the two little mice. Country Mouse had never been so frightened. He darted and dashed as fast as his aching tummy would let him. The two mice jumped through a mousehole and were safe at last in Town Mouse's house.

"Phew! I think we've done enough for one day," said Town Mouse, when they had caught their breath.

"Let's get some sleep," he said, with a yawn.
"I'll show you the rest of the house in the morning."
Country Mouse curled up in the hard little bed. But he
was too frightened and unhappy to sleep. As he listened
to his cousin snore, he tried hard not to cry.

Next morning, Town Mouse was
ready for more adventures, but
Country Mouse had had more
than enough. "Thank you for
inviting me," he told his cousin,
"but I have seen all I want to
see of the Big City. It is too big and
noisy and dirty – and too full of danger for
me. I want to go back to my quiet, peaceful home in the country."

So, Country
Mouse went back
to his snug, cosy
home under the
oak tree. He had
never been so
happy to see his
friends – and
they wanted to
hear all about
his adventures.
Country Mouse was
pleased to tell them
everything that
had happened in
the Big City – but
he *never, ever* went
back there again!

Mermaid Marina

In a magical cave, down at the bottom of the deep blue sea, lives Marina, a beautiful mermaid with a shimmering tail. She glides through the water, searching for shiny pearls and sparkling shells.

Coral the dolphin is Marina's very best friend. They love to twirl and dive through the crystal blue waters, and play hide-and-seek amongst the colourful seaweed.

Today there is great excitement at the bottom of the sea. It's the Sea King's birthday and there will be a party.

Marina is getting ready. She puts on a pretty necklace made from glistening pearls, a bracelet and some tiny starfish earrings.

234

MERMAID MARINA

"How do I look, Coral?" she asks her friend. Coral flaps her fins and does a special dolphin twirl – Marina looks wonderful! Finally, the mermaid brushes her beautiful long hair and weaves some tiny blue sea-flowers into it. Then, with a flick of their tails, Marina and Coral head off for the party.

When they arrive at the palace, the other mermaids are amazed – Marina looks so pretty!

"Happy Birthday, Your Majesty!" she says, and gives the king her present – a precious pearl.

"Thank you, Marina," says the king, "it's almost as lovely as you are."

A Swarm of Bees in May

A swarm of bees in May
  Is worth a load of hay;
A swarm of bees in June
  Is worth a silver spoon;
A swarm of bees in July
  Is not worth a fly.

Bow, Wow, Wow

Bow, wow, wow,
  Whose dog art thou?
"Little Tom Tinker's dog,
  Bow, wow, wow."

Incey Wincey Spider

Incey Wincey spider
  Climbing up the spout;
Down came the rain
  And washed the spider out.
Out came the sunshine
  And dried up all the rain;
Incey Wincey spider
  Climbing up again.

Tinker, Tailor

Tinker, tailor,
  Soldier, sailor,
Rich man, poor man,
  Beggarman, thief!

The Cold Old House

I know a house, and a cold old house,
　　A cold old house by the sea.
If I were a mouse in that cold old house
　　What a cold, cold mouse I'd be!

Hickory, Dickory, Dock

Hickory, dickory, dock,
　　The mouse ran up the clock.
The clock struck one,
　　The mouse ran down,
Hickory, dickory, dock.

Bat, Bat

Bat, Bat, come under my hat,
　　And I'll give you a slice of bacon,
And when I bake I'll give you a cake,
　　If I am not mistaken.

Three Blind Mice

Three blind mice, three blind mice!
　　See how they run, see how they run!
They all ran after the farmer's wife,
　　Who cut off their tails with a carving-knife,
Did ever you see such a thing in your life,
　　As three blind mice?

The Naughty Kitten

Ginger was a naughty little kitten. He didn't always mean to be naughty, but somehow things just turned out that way.

"You really should be more careful," warned Mummy. But Ginger was too busy getting into trouble to listen.

One day, Ginger was in a particularly playful mood. First, he tried to play tag with his smallest sister – and chased her right up an old apple tree. It took Daddy all morning to get her down.

Then, Ginger dropped cream all over the dog's tail. The dog whirled round and round as he tried to lick it off. He got so dizzy that he fell right over. That really made Ginger laugh until his sides hurt.

After that, Ginger thought it would be fun to play hide-and-seek with the mice – and frightened them so much that they refused to come out of their hole for the rest of the day.

Then, Ginger crept up behind the rabbit and shouted, "HI!" The poor rabbit was so surprised that he fell head-first into his breakfast. Ginger thought he looked ever so funny covered in lettuce leaves and carrots.

For his next trick, Ginger knocked over a wheelbarrow full of apples while he was trying to fly like a bird. He really couldn't help laughing when the apples knocked his little brother flying into the air.

And when one of the apples splashed into the garden pond, Ginger decided to go apple bobbing. How he laughed as the goldfish bumped into each other in their hurry to get out of his way.

Ginger laughed so much that, WHO-OO-AH! he began to lose his balance. He stopped laughing as he tried to stop himself falling into the pond. But, SPLASH! It was no good – he fell right in.

"Help! I can't swim," wailed Ginger, splashing wildly around. But he needn't have worried, the water only reached up to his knees.

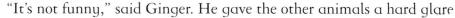

"Yuck!" he moaned, squirting out a mouthful of water.

"Ha, ha, ha!" laughed the other kittens, who had come to see what the noise was about. And the dog and the rabbit soon joined in.

"You really should be more careful," said Mummy, trying not to smile.

"It's not funny," said Ginger. He gave the other animals a hard glare as Daddy pulled him out of the pond. But then he caught sight of his reflection in the water. He did look very funny. Soon he was laughing as loudly as the others.

After that, Ginger tried hard not to be quite so naughty. And do you know what? He even succeeded... some of the time!

Trunk Trouble

Emma, Ellen and Eric Elephant had spent nearly all day at the river, splashing and sploshing in the cool, clear water and giving each other excellent elephant showers. But now it was nearly dinner time, and their rumbling tummies told them it was time to head for home.

First the little elephants had to dry themselves off. They made their way out to the clearing, and carefully dusted themselves with fine earth and sand. WHOOSH! WHOOSH! PUFFLE! went Ellen and Emma with their trunks. Both sisters had long, graceful trunks, and they were very proud of them. WHOOSH! PUFFLE! WHOOSH PUFF! went Eric, when his sisters' backs were turned. COUGH! COUGH! AH-CHOO! went Emma and Ellen. "Hey! Cut it out!" they shouted.

Eric giggled – he loved annoying his sisters. "I'll race you home!" Eric called. "Last one back is an elephant egg!" as he loped off to the jungle.

Ellen and Emma ran after him. "We'll get there first! We'll beat you!" they cried, going as quickly as they could. Ellen and Emma were running so fast and trying so hard to catch up that they forgot to look where they were going. All at once, Emma's feet got caught in a vine, and she lost her balance.

"Oh-oh-OOOOHHHH!" she cried as she slipped and staggered.

"Grab my trunk!" Ellen cried, reaching out. But Emma grabbed her sister's trunk so hard that she pulled Ellen down with her and their trunks got twisted together in a great big tangle.

"Help!" they cried. "Eric! Help!" Their brother came bounding back.

"Don't worry!" he called. "I'll save you!" Eric reached out with his trunk to try to help his sisters up. But the vine leaves were very slippery, and, as he grabbed his sisters' trunks, he slipped and lost his balance, too. Now Eric's trunk was all tangled up with Emma's and Ellen's! The three elephants sat there in a sad, tangled heap. They could barely move.

"What are we going to do?" wailed Emma.

"Don't worry, someone will come and help us," Ellen said, hopefully.

"This is all your fault!" Eric grumbled. "If it wasn't for you two, I'd be home now, eating my dinner!"

A moment later, Seymour Snake came slithering by. "Isss thisss an interesting new game?" he hissed, looking at the heap of elephants.

"No!" sobbed Emma. "We're all tangled together and we can't get up. Can you help us, Seymour?"

"Well I'll ccccertainly do my besssssst," said Seymour. "Let's sssee if I can untwissst you." He wriggled in amongst the tangle of trunks to see what he could do.

But everything was so muddled and jumbled together that Seymour couldn't even find his way out! "GRACIOUSSS ME!" he exclaimed. "I SSSEEM TO BE SSSSTUCK!"

"Great!" said Eric. "Now we have a snake to worry about, too!"

"I ssssuggest you sssstart thinking about a ssssolution to all thissss," Seymour hissed. "I'm not too tangled up to give you a nasssty nip!"

Just then Mickey and Maxine Monkey swung through the branches.

"HEY, YOU GUYS!" they shouted. They weren't very far away – Mickey and Maxine always shouted. "WHAT'S GOING ON?"

"We're stuck!" cried Ellen. "Please untangle us so we can go home!"

"Well, we can try pulling you apart," said Maxine, scurrying down. "Mickey, you take a tail, and I'll take some ears."

Mickey grabbed hold of Eric's tail and Maxine gripped Ellen's ears. Then they both pulled and pulled and p-u-l-l-e-d.

"OUCH-OUCH-OOUUCCHH!" bellowed Ellen. "I'm being ssssqueezzzed breathlesssss!" hissed Seymour in alarm.

Mickey and Maxine gave up. Pulling clearly wasn't going to work.

Suddenly there was a flapping up above as Portia Parrot and her daughter Penelope flew above with something in their beaks. As everyone looked up, they let it go and a large cloud of dry, dusty, earth drifted downwards.

"Cough-cough-ca-choooo!" spluttered Mickey and Maxine.

TRUNK TROUBLE

"Cough-cough-ca-choooo!" thundered the elephants. At first, they didn't know what had happened. Then they realised – they had sneezed themselves apart!

"Thank you," cried the elephants and Seymour.

"Happy to help!" said Portia.

"Everyone's invited to our house for dinner!" said Eric.

"Hooray!" cried the others.

With their trunks held high, the elephants led the way – walking calmly and very, very carefully!

The Princess of Hearts

Princess Ruby was given her name because she was born with ruby red lips the shape of a tiny heart. When she grew up she was very beautiful, with coal black hair down to her waist, green eyes and skin as pale as milk. She was a charming and friendly girl, but she insisted that everything she owned was heart-shaped! Her bed was heart-shaped, her table and chair were heart-shaped, even the sandwiches her maid brought her at teatime were cut into the shape of hearts!

As soon as she was old enough, the king and queen wanted Princess Ruby to find a husband. "There is a prince in the next kingdom who is looking for a wife," they told her. "He is brave and handsome and rich. Everything a princess could wish for."

But the foolish princess declared: "I will only marry this prince if he can change the stars in the sky to hearts!"

When Prince Gallant came to visit Princess Ruby she liked his kindly eyes and his pleasant smile. They spent the afternoon walking in the palace gardens, and talking about everything under the sun. But Prince Gallant could not promise to change the stars. As she watched the prince ride away, Princess Ruby suddenly wished she had not been so foolish!

Prince Gallant, too, was unhappy as he rode home. Suddenly, he heard a screeching sound. In the forest clearing, a dragon was attacking a peacock.

The prince took out his sword and chased the dragon away. The peacock's beautiful tail feathers were lying around him.

"Thank you for saving me," said the peacock. The prince was astonished to hear the peacock talk. "I have magical powers," explained the peacock. "But I am now very weak. The dragon has pulled out some of my magic feathers!"

The Prince set to work gathering up all the peacock's feathers. As soon as the feathers had been returned, the peacock gave a loud cry and spread his tail wide. The peacock's tail glowed.

"Before I go, I will grant you a single wish," he told the prince. Prince Gallant wished that the stars in the sky would take on the shape of hearts!

Later that night Princess Ruby was in her bedchamber. She was beginning to regret that she had refused to marry Prince Gallant.

She looked out of the window at the full moon and fields beyond the palace. Then she glanced at the stars — and couldn't believe her eyes!

Every single one was in the shape of a silver heart!

At that moment she saw Prince Gallant riding over the hill. He stopped his horse beneath Princess Ruby's window.

The prince again asked Princess Ruby if she would marry him. And of course she happily agreed!

They were married on a lovely summer's day. And, when Princess Ruby made her wedding vows, she promised never to ask for anything foolish, ever again!

A Windy Day

I
t was a bright and breezy morning at Faraway Farm. Rosie looked out of her bedroom window. "Come and look, Mum," she called. "The clouds are like big fluffy sheep running across blue grass."

"Mmm, it looks like a good day for hanging out the washing," said Mum. "It will soon dry in a breeze like this."

Rosie and Danny helped Mum sort out all the washing. There were sheets and towels, shirts and socks, Danny's muddy football jersey, Rosie's best party dress... Dad's stripy jumper and the yellow spotty rug that Conker the dog slept on. "Billy Rabbit needs a bath," said Rosie. "His ears are dirty and he's spilt cocoa all down his jacket."

"It was you that spilt cocoa down his jacket," laughed Danny.

"I only asked him if he wanted a little sip," replied Rosie.

Mum put on the radio and sang along with the music. Rosie put in

the washing powder and Danny turned the knobs. Conker got under everyone's feet and Stan the cat kept trying to sleep in the washing basket. The last thing to go in was Billy Rabbit.

The washing was soon done. Mum carried the basket full of heavy wet clothes. Rosie carried Billy. He was now beautifully clean but dripping wet. "We'll hang Billy on the line, too," said Mum. "He'll be dry in no time!"

When they went outside, the wind was blowing hard. Joe, the farm worker, was trying to mend the gate and hold on to his hat at the same time! "Ooh, look at the cloud sheep," cried Rosie. "They are really running fast now!"

"I should peg that washing on tight if I were you," shouted Joe. "The wind is getting stronger and stronger. Mick can't get his milk

lorry through because there's a fallen tree across the road." The sheets billowed like the sails of a ship, the socks bounced up and down and Dad's stripy jumper looked as though it had somebody inside it. Danny spread his arms wide and ran around the yard pretending to be an aeroplane.

"Whee! I love windy days!" he cried.

"Billy Rabbit is dancing on the line," exclaimed Rosie.

"Come on. Inside, you two," ordered Mum.

The wind got stronger and stronger. It rattled the windows and made whistling noises under the door. "Look, here comes, Jack!" cried Rosie. "Oops! The wind has blown off his hat!"

"Oh dear," said Mum. "I think we had better check the washing."

Whoooosh! The wind nearly knocked them over when they went outside. "Help! I'm being blown awaaaay!" shouted Rosie.

"So are all Jack's letters. Look. They are all over the lane," said Danny.

"Mum!" gasped Danny. "Where's the washing gone? Where's my football jersey?"

"Where's my Billy?" wailed Rosie. There were sheets in the hedges, socks in the duck pond and letters all over the lane. Dad's stripy jumper was halfway up the apple tree.

"Here's my football jersey," shouted Danny. "It's muddier than when I played in it."

Conker found his spotty rug and sat down on it to stop it blowing in with the chickens. "Well, that's about the lot," said Mum. "Quick, let's take it inside before the wind gets it again."

"It looks as if Jack found all his letters," said Danny.

"But where's my Billy?" sobbed Rosie.

"Come and look at this," called Joe. "The little piglets have found a new friend." Right in the middle of the pig pen sat Billy Rabbit. The piglets were squealing with excitement and twirling their curly tails.

"Oh there you are, you blow-away rabbit!" smiled Rosie.

"I know the piglets are very friendly but now you've got mud all over your jacket. You are a silly Billy. I'll have to give you a bath all over again."

In the Darkness

In the darkness of Ben's bedroom, something was moving. It wasn't Ben. He was fast asleep. But Ben's teddy bear was wide awake. As Ben slept, his bear slipped from the bed, crept across the floor, and out through the bedroom door.

On the landing, Ben's bear climbed on to the banister, and slid downstairs with a whoosh! Then he rode Ben's trike down the hall and into the kitchen where he clambered through the cat flap and out into the cold, dark night.

In his bedroom, Ben was still fast asleep.

In the garden, Ben's teddy bear headed for the sand-pit. He piled the sand high and patted it with his paws. He stuck a twig in the top, threaded with a leaf to look like a flag.

Then he ran across to the swing and climbed on to the seat. He began to swing to and fro, faster and faster, higher and higher, as he tried to reach the twinkling stars.

In his bedroom, Ben dreamt of all the things that he and Bear had done that day.

In the garden, Ben's bear clambered up the steps to the top of the slide. He slithered down and landed with a scrunch in the pile of leaves at the bottom.

Suddenly, he spotted two bright yellow eyes peering at him from the flower bed. The cat! Time to go! He quickly scrabbled through the cat flap, back into the safety of the kitchen.

He knew just where Ben's mum kept the honey. So, before he went back to bed, he opened the jar and dipped in his paw.

In his bedroom, Ben turned over in his sleep, and yawned. Light was creeping through the curtains. He reached out for his bear.

"That's funny," thought Ben. "I can feel sand on the sheet." He opened his eyes, sleepily. "Strange," he thought. "What's that leaf doing, stuck behind Bear's ear?" He wondered whether he should ask Bear, but his bear was fast asleep, and Ben didn't want to wake him.

Ben was feeling hungry, he needed a honey sandwich. He slipped from the bed and turned the sticky handle of his bedroom door. He didn't notice the sticky bear print on the door handle!

Jelly on the Plate

Jelly on the plate,
　Jelly on the plate,
Wibble, wobble,
　Wibble, wobble,
Jelly on the plate.

Sweeties in the jar,
　Sweeties in the jar,
Shake them up,
　Shake them up,
Sweeties in the jar.

Candles on the cake,
　Candles on the cake,
Blow them out,
　Blow them out,
Puff, PUFF, PUFF!

Polly Put the Kettle On

Polly put the kettle on,
　Polly put the kettle on,
Polly put the kettle on,
　We'll all have tea.

Sukey take it off again,
　Sukey take it off again,
Sukey take it off again,
　They've all gone away.

I Scream

I scream, you scream,
We all scream for ice cream!

Little Jack Horner

Little Jack Horner,
　Sat in a corner,
Eating a Christmas pie.
　He put in his thumb,
And pulled out a plum,
　And said, "What a good boy am I!"

Ten Green Bottles

Ten green bottles, standing on a wall,
　Ten green bottles, standing on a wall,
And if one green bottle should accidentally fall,
　There'd be nine green bottles, standing on a wall.

Nine green bottles, standing on a wall,
　Nine green bottles, standing on a wall,
　And if one green bottle should accidentally fall,
　　There'd be eight green bottles, standing on a wall.

Eight green bottles, standing on a wall,
　Eight green bottles, standing on a wall,
And if one green bottle should accidentally fall,
　There'd be seven green bottles, standing on a wall.

(continue with seven green bottles etc...)

A Peanut

A peanut sat on the railway track,
　His heart was all a-flutter;
Along came a train – the 9:15 –
　Toot, toot, peanut butter!

Pat-a-Cake

Pat-a-cake, pat-a-cake, baker's man,
　Bake me a cake, as fast as you can.
Pat it and prick it and mark it with B,
　And put it in the oven for Baby and me.

Dibbity, Dibbity, Dibbity, Doe

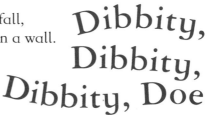

Dibbity, dibbity, dibbity, doe,
　Give me a pancake
　And I'll go.
Dibbity, dibbity, dibbity, ditter,
　Please to give me
　A bit of a fritter.

Beauty and the Beast

Once upon a time there was a man who lived in a cottage in the country with his three daughters. His youngest daughter was so pretty that everyone called her "Beauty", which made her two sisters very angry and jealous.

One day the man had to go to the city. Before he left, he told his daughters that he would bring each of them back a present and asked what they would like.

"Jewels!" the eldest daughter demanded. "Silk dresses!" said the second daughter. But all Beauty asked for was a single white rose.

On his return home, the father was caught in a snowstorm and lost his way. The blizzard was so thick and fierce and the forest so large and dark that he nearly gave up hope of ever finding his home. Then, through the mist, he glimpsed a grand palace.

He staggered to the great door – there seemed to be no one about. Inside, he found a table laid with a magnificent dinner. The man ate hungrily, then searched the house. Upstairs, he found a huge bed where he gratefully fell into an exhausted sleep. In the morning, when he awoke, breakfast was waiting beside the bed.

As he set off on his way home he noticed a wonderful rose garden. Remembering Beauty's request, he stopped to pick a white rose. Suddenly, with a mighty roar, a terrifying, snarling Beast appeared.

"I have welcomed you with every comfort," he growled, "and in return you steal my roses!"

Shaking with fear, the man begged for forgiveness. "I only wanted the rose as a present for my daughter!"

"I will spare you," said the Beast, "but only if your daughter comes to live here of her own free will. If not, you must return in three months."

Back home, the man tearfully told his daughters what had happened. To his surprise, Beauty agreed to go.

When she arrived at the palace, a glorious meal was waiting for her.

"The Beast must want to fatten me," she thought. But she sat and ate.

As soon as Beauty finished her meal, the Beast appeared. He was truly horrifying, and she was frightened.

"Your room is all ready," said the Beast, and he led her to a door that said "Beauty's Room" in gold letters.

The room was everything Beauty could have wished for. She saw a little piano, beautiful silk dresses and fresh, fragrant roses. On the dressing table was a mirror with these words on it:

If anything you long to see,
Speak your wish, and look in me.

"I wish I could see my father," said Beauty, and instantly saw her father in the mirror, sitting sadly beside the fire at home.

"Perhaps the Beast doesn't mean to kill me after all," Beauty thought. "I wonder what he does want?"

The next evening the Beast joined Beauty for supper. "Tell me," he said, "am I truly horrible to look at?"

Beauty could not lie. "You are," she said. "But I know you are very kind-hearted."

"Then," said the Beast, "will you marry me?"

Beauty was surprised. She knew he might be angry if she refused, but she couldn't say yes because she didn't love him. "No," she said, "I will not marry you."

The Beast sighed so heavily that the walls shook. "Good night, then," he said sadly. And he left her to finish her dinner alone.

Months passed, and the Beast gave Beauty

everything she could want. She was very happy in the palace.

Every evening, the Beast asked the same question: "Will you marry me?" And Beauty always said no. But she was growing very fond of him.

One day, Beauty looked in the magic mirror and saw that her father was ill. She begged the Beast to let her go home, and sadly he agreed.

"Take this magic ring," he told her. "If you ever want to come back, put it by your bedside, and when you wake up, you will be here."

"I will come back," Beauty promised.

So Beauty went home to look after her father. He was soon well again, and she was ready to go back to the Beast. But her jealous sisters hated to think of Beauty going back to a palace while they lived in a small cottage. So they convinced her to stay a while longer.

One night, Beauty dreamt that the Beast was lying dead in his garden, and she woke up in tears. She knew then that she loved the Beast, and had to return to him.

Putting the magic ring by her bedside, Beauty lay down again and closed her eyes.

When she opened them again, Beauty was back in the Beast's garden – and, true to her dream, he was lying lifeless on the ground.

"Oh, Beast," she cried, taking him in her arms, "please don't die! I love you, and I want to marry you!"

All at once light and music filled the air, and the Beast vanished. In his place stood a handsome prince.

"Who are you?" cried Beauty.

"I was your Beast," said the prince. "An evil witch cast a spell on me and turned me into that poor animal. The spell could only be broken when a beautiful girl agreed to marry me."

A few days later they were married, and Beauty's family came to join in the joyous celebrations at the palace.

Beauty had never been so happy. She loved the prince with all her heart, and they lived in their rose palace happily ever after.

The Pig and the Jewels

Daisy was as pretty as a picture, and very kind too. Daisy looked after all the animals on the farm where she lived. She loved them all dearly, and the animals all loved her, too. But Daisy dreamt of being more than a farmer's daughter, she day-dreamed about being a princess.

One day she found a sick pig at the edge of the forest. She took him to the farm and nursed him back to health. The pig became her favourite animal, and he followed her wherever she went.

She told him all her secrets, and he listened carefully, his little eyes fixed on hers. It was as if he understood everything she said. She even told him the most important secret of all.

"Dear little pig," she whispered in his ear, " I wish, I wish I could be a princess!" That night the pig went away. When he returned the next morning, he had a tiara made of precious jewels on his head.

"Darling pig," cried Daisy, "is that for me?" The pig grunted. Daisy put the tiara on her head. It fitted her perfectly.

The next night the pig went away and in the morning he returned with a beautiful necklace. Daisy put it on.

"How do I look?" she asked him. But of course the pig just grunted.

After that the pig went away every night for six nights and returned with something different. First a dress of white silk, followed by a crimson cloak and soft leather shoes. Then jewelled bracelets, and long lengths of satin ribbon for her hair. And, finally, a ring made of gold and rubies.

Daisy put on all the gifts the pig had brought her and stood in front of her mirror. "At last," she whispered, "I look just like a real princess."

The next day the pig disappeared again. Daisy didn't worry because she knew he always returned. But days went by and then weeks, and the pig did not return. Daisy missed him more than she could say.

Daisy spent the evenings sitting by the fire in her white silk dress and crimson cloak. Her heart was sad and heavy when she thought about her dear, lost pig. "I would be happy just to remain a farmer's daughter if only he would return to me," she cried, watching the logs blaze in the hearth. Suddenly there was a noise at the door. Opening it, she saw the pig!

With a cry of joy she bent to kiss him and, as she did, he turned into a handsome prince! Daisy gasped with amazement.

"Sweet Daisy," said the prince taking her hand. "If it wasn't for you I would still be alone and friendless, wandering in the forest."

He explained how a wicked witch had cast a spell to turn him into a pig. "Your kiss broke the spell," said the prince. "Daisy, will you marry me?" It was a dream come true. At long last, Daisy really was going to become Princess Daisy!

The Hare and the Tortoise

Hare was the most boastful animal in the whole forest. On this fine, sunny morning, he was trotting down the forest path singing, "I'm handsome and clever and the fastest hare ever! There's no one as splendid as me!"

Mole, Mouse and Squirrel watched him from the fallen log. "Hare is so annoying," said Mole. "Someone should find a way to stop him boasting all the time!"

"I'll get him to stop!" said Squirrel and he jumped on to the path right in front of Hare. "I'm as handsome as you are, Hare," he said. "Look at my big bushy tail."

"It's not as handsome as my fluffy white tail and my long silky ears!" boasted Hare.

"Well, I'm as clever as you are!" said Mouse, hurrying out to join them. "I can dig holes under trees and store enough nuts and seeds to last all winter!"

"That's nothing!" said Hare. "In winter, I can change my coat to white, so that I can hide in the snow!"

THE HARE AND THE TORTOISE

"Now, is there anyone who thinks they can run as *fast* as me?" said Hare to the animals, who had gathered round. "Who wants a race?" No one said anything! All the animals knew that Hare was *very fast* and no one thought they could beat him. "Ha!" exclaimed Hare. "That proves it! I'm the handsomest, the cleverest *and* the fastest."

"Excuse me," said a small voice.

"Yes?" said Hare, turning around.

"I will race you," said Tortoise.

"YOU?" said Hare, in amazement. "The slowest, clumsiest animal on four legs?"

"Yes," said Tortoise, quietly. "I will race you." The other animals gasped and Hare roared with laughter.

"Will you race me to the willow tree?" Hare asked Tortoise.

"Yes," said Tortoise.

"Will you race past the willow tree, to the stream?" asked Hare.

"Yes, I will," said Tortoise.

"Will you race past the willow tree, past the stream and all the way to the old oak tree?" asked Hare.

"Of course I will," said Tortoise.

"Fine," said Hare. "We'll start at nine o'clock in the morning! We'll meet here, at the big oak tree."

"All right," said Tortoise. The other animals ran off to tell their friends the news.

The next morning, everyone had turned out to watch the big race. Some were at the starting line and others were going to the finish, to see who would get there first.

Magpie called, "Ready, steady, GO!" And Tortoise and Hare were off! Hare shot past Tortoise and, when there was no one to show off for, he slowed down just a bit. He reached the willow tree and looked behind him – Tortoise was not in sight!

"It will take him ages just to catch me," Hare thought. "I don't need to hurry. I may as well stop and rest." He sat down under the willow tree and closed his eyes. In minutes, he was fast asleep.

Meanwhile, Tortoise just plodded on. He didn't try to go faster than he could, but he didn't stop, either. He just kept going, on and on and on. The sun climbed higher in the sky and Tortoise felt hot. But he still kept going. His stubby legs were beginning to ache, but he knew he mustn't stop.

Hare kept snoring under the willow tree.

Some time later, Tortoise reached Hare. First of all, Tortoise thought he should wake Hare up. Then he changed his mind. "Hare is very clever," he told himself. "He must have a reason for sleeping. He would only be cross if I woke him!" So, Tortoise left Hare sleeping and went on his way, walking slowly towards the finish line.

The Hare and the Tortoise

Later that afternoon, as the sun began to sink and the air grew chilly, Hare awoke with a start. "The race!" he thought. "I have to finish the race!" He looked around to see if Tortoise was nearby. There was no sign of him. "Hah!" said Hare. "He still hasn't caught up with me. No need to hurry, then."

And he trotted towards the clearing, with a big grin on his face. When he neared the finish, Hare could hear cheers and clapping. "They must be able to see me coming," he thought. But, as he got closer, he saw the real reason for all the noise and his heart sank. There was Tortoise, crossing the line. Tortoise had won! The animals were cheering wildly. As Hare crept up to the finishing line, the cheers turned to laughter. His ears turned bright red and drooped with embarrassment. Hare moped off and everyone gathered round to congratulate Tortoise, who looked shy, but very proud. He had proved that slow but steady always wins the race.

Somehow the animals knew that they wouldn't have to listen to Hare's loud, annoying boasting any more!

The Princess who Never Smiled

A long time ago, in a far off land, a princess was born. The king and queen called her Princess Columbine. They thought she was the most precious child ever to be born. And, to make sure that she was watched over every minute of every day, they hired a nurse to look after her.

One day the queen came to the nursery and found the nurse asleep and the little princess crying. The queen was very cross and called for the king who told off the nurse for not watching the baby.

But what the king and queen didn't know was that the nurse was really a wicked enchantress, and she cast a spell over the baby princess:

"Princess Columbine will not smile again until she learns my real name!"

The king and queen were devastated. From that day on, the princess never smiled! Names were collected from all over the land. They tried all the usual names such as Jane, Catherine, Amanda. They tried more unusual names such as Araminta, Tallulah, Leanora. They even tried quite outlandish names such as Dorominty, Truditta, Charlottamina. But none broke the spell.

Princess Columbine grew up to be a sweet and beautiful girl. Everybody loved her. But her face was always so sad, it made the king and queen unhappy. They tried everything to make her smile. They bought her a puppy. They even hired a court jester who told the silliest jokes you've ever heard.

"Why did the pecans cross the road?" asked the jolly jester. The princess shrugged.

"Because they were nuts!" the jester guffawed.

"Why did the ice cream?" the jester tried again. The princess just gazed politely.

"Because the jelly wobbled!"

One day an artist called Rudolpho came to the palace and asked the king if he could paint the princess's portrait. The king agreed on condition that he painted the princess smiling. Rudolpho set up his easel beneath a large mirror and began painting. The princess sat opposite watching him paint in the mirror behind him. He had soon painted the princess's portrait, all except for her smile.

Rudolpho tried some funny drawings to make the princess smile. He drew silly pictures of the king and queen while the princess looked on politely. Then he drew a picture of her old nurse and gave her a moustache, and underneath he wrote NURSE.

Princess Columbine gazed at the picture in the mirror. There, underneath the picture, was the word NURSE spelled out back to front. "ESRUN," Princess Columbine said quietly. And then she smiled.

"Her name is ESRUN!" laughed Princess Columbine. At last the spell was broken! When the king and queen heard her laughter they rushed to see what was happening. Everyone was so happy that soon they were all laughing too — but Princess Columbine laughed the loudest.

See a Pin and Pick It Up

See a pin and pick it up,
  All the day you'll have good luck;
See a pin and let it lay,
  Bad luck you'll have all the day!

Miss Mary Mack

Miss Mary Mack, Mack, Mack,
  All dressed in black, black, black,
With silver buttons, buttons, buttons,
  All down her back, back, back.
She went upstairs to make her bed,
  She made a mistake and bumped her head;
She went downstairs to wash the dishes,
  She made a mistake and washed her wishes;
She went outside to hang her clothes,
  She made a mistake and hung her nose.

Ring-a-Ring o'Roses

Ring-a-ring o'roses,
  A pocket full of posies,
A-tishoo! A-tishoo!
  We all fall down!

Mr Nobody

Mr Nobody is a nice young man,
  He comes to the door with his hat in his hand.
Down she comes, all dressed in silk,
  A rose in her bosom, as white as milk.
She takes off her gloves, she shows me her ring,
  Tomorrow, tomorrow, the wedding begins.

Little Sally Waters

Little Sally Waters,
    Sitting in the sun,
Crying and weeping,
    For a young man.
Rise, Sally, rise,
    Dry your weeping eyes,
Fly to the east,
    Fly to the west,
Fly to the one you love the best.

Oliver Twist

Oliver Twist
    You can't do this,
So what's the use
    Of trying?
Touch your toe,
    Touch your knee,
Clap your hands,
    Away we go.

Three Children

Three children sliding on the ice
    Upon a winter's day,
As it fell out, they all fell in,
    The rest they ran away.

Now had these children been at home,
    Or sliding on dry ground,
Ten thousand pounds to one penny
    They had not all been drowned.

You parents all that children have,
    And you that have got none,
If you would have them safe abroad,
    Pray keep them safe at home.

Georgie, Porgie

Georgie, Porgie, pudding and pie,
    Kissed the girls and made them cry;
When the boys came out to play
    Georgie Porgie ran away.

Lion

It was Lion's birthday.
"The animals must have forgotten," said Lion. "No one has wished me happy birthday."

Lion walked slowly through the jungle, feeling very sad.

"Let's surprise Lion with a birthday party!" said Elephant.

"We'll bring our birthday presents," said Giraffe…

…"and we will think of lots of games to play," said Monkey.

"We'll dance and have fun," said Zebra.

"HAPPY BIRTHDAY, LION!" called Hippo.

"Happy birthday!" sang the animals.

"What a SURPRISE!" roared Lion.

The animals had fun all afternoon, it was the best party ever!

Monkey

Tiny Monkey looked sad. He did not know how to climb.

The animals decided they would try to cheer him up.

"I'll bring some leaves to shade you from the sun," said Giraffe.

"I will bring feathers to make a cosy bed for you," said Parrot.

"And a long bedtime story will help you to sleep," yawned Lion.

"But I don't want to sleep," said Tiny Monkey. "I want to learn to climb."

"I will teach you, Tiny Monkey," said Big Monkey.

"Just follow me. Cling with your feet, and swing your tail – like this!"

Taking a deep breath, Tiny Monkey raced up the tree, clinging to the branches.

"Look at me! I'm the best climbing monkey in the forest!" he called.

Missing Mouse

In some ways, Molly Mouse was just like her brother and sisters. She had soft, pink ears and a cute, little nose. But, in other ways, she was very different...

Milly, Max and Baby Mouse were very tidy, but Molly was really, really messy! Her whiskers were never clean and her paws were always grubby. And, everywhere Molly went, she left a messy muddle behind her!

After breakfast, Milly and Max never forgot to make their beds. Each and every morning, they threw out their old bedding and made new beds with fresh, clean hay. But Molly wasn't bothered! She just jumped out of bed and left everything in a tangled, untidy heap!

"How can you sleep in that mess?" asked Milly, her sister.

At lunch time, the rest of the family nibbled their food carefully and always cleaned up after themselves. They brushed up their crumbs and cleared away their bowls. But Molly wasn't bothered! She just munched away merrily, scattering food everywhere!

MISSING MOUSE

"Why do you make such a mess?" asked Daddy Mouse.

At playtime, Milly and Max would carefully scamper up cornstalks. But Molly couldn't be bothered! She rushed up the stalks so fast, that she snapped them in two and fell to the ground in a messy heap!

"Why are you so clumsy?" asked Max.

And when Max and Milly collected nuts and seeds for their tea, they always stacked them in neat, little piles. But Molly couldn't be bothered! Her heaps always toppled over.

"Why are you so untidy?" asked Milly.

Everyone was really fed up with Molly and her messy ways. "Why can't you eat properly?" said Daddy Mouse.

"Why can't you keep yourself clean and tidy?" said Mummy Mouse.

"Why can't you be quieter?" said Baby Mouse.

"Oh, Molly," groaned Milly and Max.

"I can't do anything right," Molly sniffed. "It's not fair." And, with her messy tail in her paw, she said "Goodnight" and went to bed.

But Molly had a plan. She was fed up with all the grumbling and she wasn't going to put up with it any longer! So, when Max and Milly came to bed, Molly was already fast asleep – at least, that's what they thought. Molly was really wide awake!

She waited until her brother and sister were asleep and then crept out of bed. "No one loves me," she sighed. "I think I'll go and find somewhere else to live." So, off she set!

Molly had no idea where she was going. She scurried along the hedgerow and scampered through the cornstalks. And, as the sun began to rise, she slipped out of the field and happily skipped down the lane.

"I'll show them!" she said. "Why should I stay at home to be grumbled and moaned at? I'm going to find a home where people want me."

But, as the morning went on and Molly got further and further away from home, she became very tired. She sat down by a farmyard gate. "I'm really sleepy," she said, and gave a big yawn! Then Molly noticed the barn door slightly open. Inside was a warm and comfy pile of hay – perfect for a little nap! She snuggled up in the hay and fell fast, fast asleep.

Back at home, when Mummy Mouse came to wake up her little ones, Molly's bed was empty. "Where's Molly?" she asked Milly and Max.

The two little mice rubbed their eyes and looked around. "We don't know," they said. "She was here last night, fast asleep."

"Daddy! Daddy! Come quick!" called Mummy Mouse. "Our Molly's missing!" So, they searched the house, but Molly was not

there. They went outside and looked through the cornfield, combed the hedgerows, searched under and over toadstools, in fact, they didn't leave a leaf unturned! They even went down the lane.

Suddenly, Milly started jumping up and down. "Look!" she squealed, pointing at the muddy path that led into the farmyard.

There, right in front of Milly, was a set of tiny mouse footprints.

Milly and Max followed the footprints across the farmyard and into the barn. And there, fast asleep in a messy pile of hay, was Molly.

"We've found her!" they shouted.

Molly slowly opened her eyes. There were bits of straw sticking to her fur, her whiskers were crumpled and her paws were muddy. "Oh, Molly!" yelled Milly and Max. "We've missed you so much."

"How can you have missed *me*?" said Molly. "I'm always such a mess!"

"You might be messy," said her mummy, "but we love you just the same!" Everyone cheered and Molly smiled – they really did love her!

And with that, they set off home.

The Tooth Fairy

Pansy was nearly five. She couldn't wait for her birthday because Mum had promised her a party in the garden with a birthday cake, balloons and a funny clown. There was only one problem! Pansy's two front teeth were loose. They wobbled whenever she bit into anything. How was she going to enjoy her party food?

"Mum," she asked, for the hundredth time, "will my wobbly teeth come out before my birthday party?"

"They'll come out when they're ready," said Mum, smiling.

That night Pansy woke suddenly. The curtains were open and her bed was covered in silvery moonlight. But that wasn't all! Sitting on Pansy's pillow was… can you guess? A fairy! She was tiny, with pale yellow wings, a wand and a sparkly dress. Pansy could not believe it. She stared at the fairy, and the fairy stared back at her.

The fairy spoke first. "Can you see me?" she asked. "Yes," said Pansy.

"That's funny," said the little fairy. "Usually I'm invisible!" "Are you the tooth fairy?" asked Pansy.

"Yes, I'm Bobo," said the fairy. "I need two tiny front teeth to replace the keys on my piano." Pansy showed Bobo her two front teeth. They were very wobbly. "I hope they come out before my birthday party," said Pansy.

"They'll come out when they are ready," said Bobo. "If they come out in time, I'll play my piano at your party!"

At teatime Bobo watched from behind a bowl of fruit, as Pansy ate all her cheese on toast, including the crusts. Still her teeth didn't come out!

"Try brushing your teeth," Bobo whispered to her before Pansy went to bed.

"Oh yes! That will do it!" said Pansy. And she brushed and brushed, but the wobbly teeth just stayed stubbornly in her mouth.

The day before Pansy's birthday her two front teeth came out! It didn't hurt one little bit. "Look!" she said to Mum, pulling a face, and showing a big gap where her teeth should be.

That night Pansy went to bed early. She put her teeth under the pillow.

Later Bobo came in, but Pansy was fast asleep. Bobo even whispered Pansy's name, but Pansy was fast asleep. Pansy didn't wake until the sun shone through her curtains the next morning. The first thing she did was look under the pillow. The two tiny teeth had gone! In their place were two coins.

Pansy's fifth birthday party was the best she'd ever had. All her friends came. There was jelly and ice cream, balloons and the funniest clown she'd ever seen.

Her friends sang Happy Birthday so loudly that Mum had to put her fingers in her ears. But only Pansy could hear the tiny fairy playing a piano and singing Happy Birthday in a silvery voice.

A Good Example

Tilly and Old George were kind old horses, but they didn't understand the young animals who tore around the farmyard.

"Look at that piglet," Tilly grumbled one day. "He's leaving muddy trotter-prints all over the yard."

"And those noisy chicks and ducklings are not behaving very well either," neighed Old George, nodding his head in agreement. "They should know better than to cheep and quack during our afternoon nap."

"Things were very different in the old days," sighed Tilly. "Youngsters were well brought up then. When we were foals, we were tidy and very, very quiet."

Unfortunately, Tilly and Old George didn't keep their feelings to themselves...

The next morning, Tilly told Percy the pig how to discipline his piglets.

Old George gave Jenny and Henrietta the hens some advice and tips on bringing up chicks. And both the horses had a word with Doris the duck about the correct time and place for ducklings to quack.

By lunch time, there wasn't a single animal on the farmyard who wasn't feeling cross with Tilly and Old George.

"I'd like to see them look after even one little one," said Doris.

Strangely enough, it was that afternoon that Old MacDonald brought a new foal to the farm for Tilly and Old George to care for. Percy, Jenny, Henrietta and Doris looked forward to having some fun!

But the animals were disappointed. The new foal, whose name was Frances, was remarkably good. She never spilled her oats, or splashed the water in her trough. She wasn't noisy, or nosy, or naughty.

Worse still, Tilly and Old George looked terribly pleased with themselves.

"You see," Old George told Percy, "it's a matter of setting a good example. If a young animal sees her parents are quiet and sensible, she naturally copies them."

And Old George made a grand, sweeping gesture with his hoof, and his shoe, which had been a little loose lately, flew right off!

The shoe shot across the farmyard. Clang! It knocked over a bucket of pig food. Clonk! It bounced off the bucket and whizzed straight through a window and into the farmhouse. Crash!

Mrs MacDonald stormed out into the yard. She was holding an apple pie with a large horseshoe sticking in it!

"Who has done this," she cried, "and made so much noise and mess?"

Old George tried to look unconcerned and calm, but the eyes of every other animal in the farmyard were upon him. And anyway, who else had shoes that big?

These days, Tilly and Old George are not quite so quick to criticise their friends. And the story of George's flying footwear still brings a smile to everyone's face – all except for Mrs MacDonald, of course!

Forever Friends

Daisy Duckling had lots of friends but her best friend of all was Cilla Cygnet. Every day they played together, chasing each other through the reeds. "When I grow up, I'll be a beautiful swan like my mummy!" said Cilla.

"And I'll be a dull little brown duck," said Daisy. She worried that Cilla would only want to play with her pretty swan friends when she grew up.

Then one day, they were playing hide and seek when something dreadful happened. While Daisy hid amongst some large dock leaves, a sly fox crept up and snatched her in his mouth!

Before she had time to quack he was heading for his lair. But Cilla had been watching. Without hesitating she rushed after the fox and caught the tip of his long tail in her sharp beak.

As the fox spun round, she pecked him hard on the nose. His mouth dropped open and Daisy fell out. Now he was really mad and rushed at them. But Mrs Duck and Mrs Swan flew at him hissing furiously, and off he ran. Daisy couldn't thank them enough.

"That's what friends are for!" said Cilla. And Mrs Swan and Mrs Duck, who were the best of friends, could not agree more.

As I was Going to St Ives

As I was going to St Ives,
  I met a man with seven wives.
Each wife had seven sacks,
  Each sack had seven cats,
Each cat had seven kits.
  Kits, cats, sacks, and wives,
How many were going to St Ives?

The Little Turtle Dove

High in the pine tree,
  The little turtle dove
Made a little nursery
  To please her little love.

"Coo," said the turtle dove,
  "Coo," said she;
In the long, shady branches
  Of the dark pine tree.

Dickery, Dickery, Dare

Dickery, dickery, dare,
  The pig flew up in the air.
The man in brown
  Soon brought him down!
Dickery, dickery, dare.

Hey, My Kitten

Hey, my kitten, my kitten,
  And hey my kitten, my deary,
Such a sweet pet as this
  There is not far nor neary.
Here we go up, up, up,
  Here we go down, down, downy;
Here we go backwards and forwards,
  And here we go round, round, roundy.

Clap Hands

Clap hands, Daddy's coming
  Up the waggon way,
His pockets full of money
  And his hands full of clay.

Pussycat Ate the Dumplings

Pussycat ate the dumplings,
  Pussycat ate the dumplings,
Mamma stood by,
  And cried, "Oh fie!
Why did you eat the dumplings?"

There Was...

There was a girl
in our town,
Silk an' satin was
her gown,
Silk an' satin, gold an'
velvet.
Guess her name, three
times I've telled it.

The Mischievous Raven

A farmer went trotting upon his grey mare,
Bumpety, bumpety, bump!
With his daughter behind him so rosy and fair,
Lumpety, lumpety, lump!

A raven cried, "Croak!" and they all tumbled down,
Bumpety, bumpety, bump!
The mare broke her knees and the farmer his crown,
Lumpety, lumpety, lump!

The mischievous raven flew laughing away,
Bumpety, bumpety, bump!
And vowed he would serve them the same next day,
Lumpety, lumpety, lump!

Cats and Dogs

Hodley, poddley, puddle and fogs,
  Cats are to marry the poodle dogs;
Cats in blue jackets and dogs in red hats,
  What will become of the mice and the rats?

I Bought an Old Man

Hey diddle diddle,
  And hey diddle dan!
And with a little money,
  I bought an old man.
His legs were all crooked
  And wrong ways set on,
So what do you think
  Of my little old man?

Mrs White

Mrs White had a fright
  In the middle of the night.
She saw a ghost, eating toast,
  Halfway up a lamp post.

The Football Fairy

Georgina loved to play football. But there was just one problem. "I'm fed up with these silly wings," she said, wiggling her shoulders. "They just get in the way."

"Flying is brilliant, and anyway football is a game for elves, not fairies!" said Sparkle.

"In that case, I don't want to be a fairy!" said Georgina, and stamped off. "She'll change her mind," said the wise fairy, "just wait and see."

But Georgina wouldn't change her mind. She pulled on her football boots and went to play with the elves.

The football game was very rough. The ball bounced around the field and, quite often, off the field! Sometimes it went up into the trees. Two birds who were trying to build their nest got very fed up.

Georgina flew up to get it. "Perhaps my wings can be useful after all," she thought. She looked round quickly, hoping no one had seen her.

But Barry, the elf, had and he couldn't wait to tell the fairies. "Ah," nodded the wise fairy. "I knew she would use her wings sooner or later."

The next time Georgina played football, the game was rougher than ever. One elf kicked the ball so hard it flew into the tree and hit the birds' nest. This time there was an egg in it!

The egg began to topple, but none of the elves noticed;
they were far too busy arguing with the referee.

Georgina flew up and, just in time, caught the
egg before it hit the ground. Then she flew up
to the nest.

"Thank you," said the mummy bird, tucking
the egg back under her. "But please, be more
careful when you play football!"

Next time she played football, Georgina checked the tree
first. The mummy bird was away. "Good!" she thought. "She can't
complain this time." But, thanks to a naughty elf, the football knocked
into the birds' nest. A small bundle of feathers tumbled out. It was a
baby bird!

Georgina spotted it and, quick as lightening, she flew up to catch him.
Gently, she held him in her arms and flew back to the nest. When he
was safely inside she sprinkled him with fairy dust to keep him from
further harm. Just then the mummy bird came back.

"I shall tell everyone about your
kindness," she said, as her baby
snuggled under her feathers. "And,
as you're such a good fairy, will
you be baby Beak's godmother?"

"Oh, thank you! I'd be
delighted!" said Georgina.

When they heard the news, the other
fairies were very proud of her.

"Perhaps it's not so bad being a fairy after all," grinned
Georgina, happily.

Rusty's Big Day

Long ago there lived a poor farmer called Fred, who had a horse called Rusty. Once Rusty had been a good, strong horse. He had willingly pulled the plough and taken his master into town to sell his vegetables. Now he was too old to work on the farm, but the farmer couldn't bear to think of getting rid of him because he was so sweet-natured. "It would be like turning away one of my own family," Fred used to say. Rusty spent his days grazing in the corner of the field. He was quite content, but he felt sad that he was no longer able to help the poor farmer earn his living.

One day, Fred decided to go to town to sell a few vegetables. He harnessed Beauty, the young mare, to the wagon and off they went.

Beauty shook her fine mane and tossed a glance at Rusty as if to say, "Look who's queen of the farmyard!"

While Fred was in the town, his eye was caught by a notice pinned to a tree. It said:

Horse Parade at 2 pm today
The winner will pull the king's carriage to the Grand Banquet tonight

"There's not a moment to lose, my girl!" said Fred. "We must get you ready for the parade." And he turned the wagon around. "Giddy-up, Beauty!" he called, and she trotted all the way back to the farm.

Fred set to work to make Beauty look more lovely than she had ever done before. He scrubbed her hoofs and brushed her coat until it shone. Then he plaited her mane and tied it with a bright red ribbon. Rusty watched from the field. "How fine she looks," he thought, wistfully. "She's sure to win." He felt a bit sad that he was too old to take part in the parade, so he found a patch of the sweetest grass to graze on, to console himself.

All at once, he heard Fred approach. "Come on, old boy," he said, "you can come, too. It'll be fun for you to watch the parade, won't it?"

Rusty was thrilled. It was a long time since the master had last taken him into town.

Soon the three of them set off back into town, with Fred riding on Beauty's back and Rusty walking by their side. When they reached the parade ground, there were already a lot of people and horses there. There were horses of every shape and size!

The parade began. The king and members of the royal court entered the parade ground and took their places. Then the king announced three contests. First there would be a race from one end of the parade ground to the other. Then there would be a contest of strength. Each horse would have to try to pull a heavy carriage. Lastly, there would be a trotting competition. Each horse would have to carry a rider around the parade ground.

Rusty tried his best, but he couldn't compete with the younger horses in the race and the contest of strength. All the other horses stared at him. "What's an old horse like you doing taking part in a contest like this?" one of them asked disdainfully. "You shouldn't have been allowed to compete at your age!" taunted another.

Then came the trotting competition. "I shall ride each horse in turn," declared the king. He climbed up on to the first horse, but it bolted and left the king hanging by the stirrups. The next horse threw the king right up in the air! The next horse was so nervous that his teeth chattered. Then it was Beauty's turn. She carried the king magnificently, until she stumbled at the end. At last it was Rusty's turn. Rusty carried the king quite slowly and steadily, making sure he picked his feet up carefully, so that his royal highness would not be jolted. "Thank you for a most pleasant ride," said the king dismounting. There was a hush as the horses and their owners awaited the result of the contest. "I have decided," announced the king, "that Rusty is the winner. Not only did he give me a most comfortable ride, but he accepted his other defeats with dignity. Speed and strength are not everything, you know."

Rusty and Fred were overjoyed, and even Beauty offered her congratulations. "Although I probably would have won if I hadn't stumbled," she muttered.

So Rusty proudly pulled the king's carriage that evening, and he made such a good job of it that the king asked him if he would do it again the following year. Then the king asked Fred if his daughter could ride Beauty from time to time. He even gave Fred a bag of gold to pay for the horses' upkeep. So the three of them were happy as they never had been before as they returned home to the farm that night.

Princess Rosebud

In a beautiful palace in a land far away, lived a little princess. The king and queen called her Princess Rosebud, because on her left ankle was a small pink mark in the shape of a rose.

On her third birthday, the Princess Rosebud was given a pretty white pony. She rode her pony with her nanny and her groom at her side. They went to the edge of the forest, then stopped for a rest. The pretty white pony was tied to a tree branch while the nanny and the groom talked together. The little princess wandered along a forest path collecting flowers and they didn't notice her disappear. Soon Princess Rosebud was lost. She called and called for her nanny. No one came and it began to get dark. The little princess was scared and began to cry.

Princess Rosebud walked on until she saw a light through the trees. There was a little house with a straw roof and tiny little windows and a small wooden door. Suddenly, the door opened. There stood a little old woman!

Now, the old woman was blind and couldn't see the little princess, but she could hear a small child crying. She took the little princess inside and sat her by a warm fire. Then she gave her thin slices of bread and honey, and a glass of milk.

"What is your name, child?" she asked.

"Rosebud," replied the princess. "I got lost in the forest."

"Well, you can stay with me until someone comes to find you, my dear," said the kind old woman.

PRINCESS ROSEBUD

Back at the palace, the king and queen were very upset that their only daughter was lost. They offered a reward of a hundred gold coins to anyone who could find her. But many years went by and no one found the little princess. The king and queen thought they would never see the princess again.

Meanwhile Rosebud was very happy living in the forest. She forgot that she had ever been a princess and had lived in a palace! She even forgot her white pony!

One day, when she was walking in the garden, a pony appeared. He was as white as milk, with a jewelled saddle and bridle. Rosebud loved him immediately! She climbed into the saddle, and the pony galloped off. He took her to the palace gate. Rosebud felt she had seen the palace before, but could not remember. The pony trotted through the gate as the king and queen were walking in the gardens. When they saw the little girl they thought she was the prettiest girl they had ever seen.

Just as Rosebud was mounting the pony to ride home, the queen saw, to her surprise, the pink rose on her left ankle!

"Sire!" she cried to the king. "It is our daughter, Princess Rosebud."

Rosebud realised where she was, and that the king and queen were her parents. She explained where she had been living and how the old woman had looked after her. The old woman was offered a reward for caring for the princess, but she said, "I only want to be near Rosebud for the rest of my days." So the old woman came to live in the palace with Princess Rosebud.

Gym
Giraffe

Jeremy Giraffe loved going out with his dad to gather the juicy green leaves for their dinner.

"This is where the most delicious leaves are," said Dad, reaching w-a-a-a-y up to a very high branch. "Remember the tallest trees have the tastiest leaves, and the tiny top leaves are the tenderest!"

One morning, Jeremy decided it was time to gather leaves on his own. "The tallest trees have the tastiest leaves," he whispered to himself, "and the tiny top leaves are the tenderest."

Jeremy stopped at a very tall tree and looked up. There at the top were some tiny, tender, tasty-looking leaves. Str - e - e - e - e - etching his neck just as he had seen his dad do, Jeremy reached as high as he could. It wasn't very high! "Oh, no," he thought. "How will I reach the tiny, tasty top leaves if my neck won't stretch?"

So Jeremy went back home with his neck hanging down in despair.

"Why, Jeremy, what's wrong?" asked his mum. When Jeremy told her, she gave his neck a nuzzle. "Your neck's still growing," she assured him. "Eat your greens and get lots of sleep, and you'll soon be able to reach the tastiest, tenderest leaves on the tallest trees in the jungle!"

That afternoon, Jeremy went out to try again. Portia Parrot saw Jeremy struggling to reach the top of the tree. Trying to be helpful, she swooped down and plucked a few of the tenderest leaves for him.

When Portia gave Jeremy the leaves, his spots went pale with shame and embarrassment.

"I should be able to get those myself," he wailed. "Why won't my neck stretch?"

"Oh, Jeremy," said Portia, "your neck is just fine! Keep eating your greens and getting lots of sleep, and it will grow!"

"But I can't wait," Jeremy insisted. "Isn't there anything I can do to stretch my neck now?"

"Perhaps there is," said Portia, thoughtfully. "Follow me!"

Portia led Jeremy through the jungle to a clearing. Jeremy's eyes widened with wonder at what he saw. There was so much going on! Seymour Snake was wrapping himself round a fallen tree trunk. "Hello, Jeremy," he hissed. "Jusssssst doing my sssssslithering exercisesssss!"

Emma, Ellen and Eric Elephant were hoisting logs. "Hi, Jeremy," they called. "This is our trunk-strengthening workout!"

In the river, Claudia Crocodile was breaking thick branches in half. "Just limbering up my jaw muscles," she snapped.

Leonard Lion was taking his cubs, Louis and Lisa, through their pouncing paces. "Welcome to the Jungle Gym!" he called.

A few minutes later, Grandpa Gorilla and Leonard Lion came to greet Jeremy.

"What can we do for you?" they asked.

"Can you help me stretch my neck?" asked Jeremy. "I want to be able to reach the tasty, tiny, tender leaves."

"You're still growing," said Leonard Lion. "You just have to eat your greens and get lots of sleep."

Jeremy's face fell, until Grandpa Gorilla said, "But we will help things along with some special neck-stretching exercises. Come with us!"

Grandpa got Jeremy started right away.

"S-t-r-e-t-c-h to the left! S-t-r-e-t-c-h to the right!" Grandpa Gorilla shouted. "Chin lifts next," said Leonard Lion.

Jeremy s-t-r-e-e-e-t-c-h-e-d his neck to reach the branch.

"Come on, you can do it!" Portia said, cheering him on. Grandpa Gorilla told Jeremy to lie down. Then he called Seymour Snake. "Start slithering!" he said.

"Aaaaakkkk!" gasped Jeremy, as Seymour wrapped himself round his neck. "Not so tight," said Grandpa.

"That's better!" said Jeremy, as Seymour slithered along, pu-u-u-l-l-ing his neck muscles. All the exercise made Jeremy hungry.

At supper, he had three BIG helpings of greens. He was tired, too, so he went to bed early and slept soundly.

Jeremy loved the Jungle Gym and couldn't wait to go back. After his workout each day, Jeremy ate a good supper.

"Exercising makes me soooo hungry…" he said, "…and soooo tired," he yawned, as he fell asleep.

GYM GIRAFFE

The next time Jeremy and his dad went out leaf-gathering together, Jeremy spotted some sweet-looking leaves right at the top of a tall tree.

"I'm going to get those," he said.

"They're so high up!" said Dad.

Jeremy didn't hear him. He was too busy stretching… and stretching… and stretching… until he stretched right up to the very top branch!

"I've done it, Dad!" he cried happily. "The exercises worked!"

"I don't think it matters," said his mum. "What matters is that you have a fine, strong, long neck that any giraffe would be proud of!"

"And I am!" said Jeremy, taking another mouthful of tasty, tender leaves. He chewed the leaves extra thoroughly – because he knew they had a very long way to go!

Susie and the Mermaid

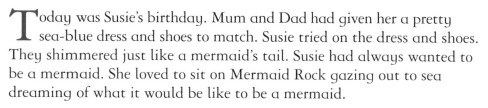

Today was Susie's birthday. Mum and Dad had given her a pretty sea-blue dress and shoes to match. Susie tried on the dress and shoes. They shimmered just like a mermaid's tail. Susie had always wanted to be a mermaid. She loved to sit on Mermaid Rock gazing out to sea dreaming of what it would be like to be a mermaid.

"I'll make a birthday wish," thought Susie, and closed her eyes. "I wish I could be a mermaid." When she opened her eyes, she was no longer wearing her birthday dress – she had a mermaid's tail! Susie couldn't believe her luck, her birthday wish had come true.

Then Susie heard someone crying. She looked around and saw someone sitting on the other side of Mermaid Rock wearing a blue dress just like her new birthday dress! "Why are you crying?" Susie asked the little girl.

"Because I've lost my tail," she replied. "You see, I'm a mermaid. But without my tail I can't go home!" Susie realised what had happened, her birthday wish must have made her swap places with the mermaid. Susie told the mermaid about her birthday wish.

"How can I change us back again?" asked Susie.

"If you can collect my tears from the sea, then you could wish again," said the mermaid.

Susie slipped into the sea. The water didn't feel a bit cold now that she was a mermaid. With her strong new tail she swam quickly to the bottom of the sea.

Susie asked the sea creatures to help her search for the tears. Crabs and fish, lobsters and winkles peered into holes and lifted up stones, but it was no use. They couldn't find any tears. Susie didn't know what to do!

Then she heard, "One-two-three, one-two-three…" and from an underwater cave danced a large octopus wearing a long string of pearls! Its eight long arms whirled around as it danced and twirled.

"Hello, little mermaid!" said the octopus. "Can you help me?" asked Susie. "I'm looking for mermaid tears. But I don't know where to start."

"Ah! Well these pearls are just what you are looking for!" said the octopus. "That's what happens to mermaid tears you know – they turn into pearls! You can have them if you help me take them off!" laughed the octopus. "Oh, thank you so much!" cried Susie untangling the pearls.

"Farewell, little mermaid!" laughed the octopus as it danced away, singing, "One-two-three, one-two-three…"

Susie swam back to Mermaid Rock as quickly as she could with the pearls. Susie closed her eyes and wished again. Instantly, she was wearing her blue dress and the mermaid had her tail back.

"Thank you, Susie," said the mermaid. "I hope I'll see you again."

Susie waved goodbye as the mermaid slipped into the sea and swam away. Susie hurried home for her birthday tea. She glanced down at her new blue dress to make sure it was still clean. Down the front of the dress were sewn lots of tiny tear-shaped pearls!

Hearts, Like Doors

Hearts, like doors, will open with ease
  To very, very, little keys,
And don't forget that two of these
  Are "I thank you" and "If you please".

Mother Shuttle

Old Mother Shuttle
Lived in a coal-scuttle
Along with her dog and her cat;
  What they ate I can't tell,
  But 'tis known very well
That not one of the party was fat.

Little Husband

I had a little husband,
  No bigger than my thumb;
I put him in a pint pot
  And there I bade him drum.
I gave him some garters
  To garter up his hose,
And a little silk handkerchief
  To wipe his pretty nose.

Rumpty-iddity

Rumpty-iddity, row, row, row,
If I had a good supper,
I could eat it now.

Willy Boy

Willy boy, Willy boy,
  Where are you going?
I will go with you,
  If that I may.
I'm going to the meadow
  To see them a-mowing,
I am going to help them
  Turn the new hay.

Two Little Dogs

Two little dogs
  Sat by the fire
Over a fender of coal-dust;
  Said one little dog
  To the other little dog,
If you don't talk, why, I must.

The Robins

A robin and a robin's son
  Once went to town to buy a bun.
They couldn't decide on a plum or plain,
  And so they went back home again.

The Merchants of London

Hey diddle dinkety, poppety, pet,
   The merchants of London they wear scarlet;
Silk in the collar and gold in the hem,
   So merrily march the merchant men.

The Dame of Dundee

There was an old woman,
   Who lived in Dundee,
And in her back garden
   There was a plum tree;
The plums they grew rotten
   Before they grew ripe,
And she sold them
   Three farthings a pint.

Christmas Eve

On Christmas Eve I turned the spit,
   I burnt my fingers, I feel it yet;
The little cock sparrow flew over the table,
   The pot began to play with the ladle.

Gingerbread Men

Smiling girls, rosy boys,
   Come and buy my little toys;
Monkeys made of gingerbread,
   And sugar horses painted red.

First

First in a carriage,
   Second in a gig,
Third on a donkey,
   And fourth on a pig.

The Wedding

Pussycat, wussicat, with a white foot,
   When is your wedding and I'll come to it.
The beer's to brew, and the bread's to bake,
   Pussycat, wussicat, don't be too late.

Bears Ahoy!

O ne summer's day,
three little boys
went for a picnic by the
bank of a river. They took with
them their swimming things, some cheese and pickle sandwiches and,
of course, their teddy bears.

When they arrived, they found a small boat tied to a tree. The
boys climbed on board, taking their teddies with them, and had a
great game of pirates. The boys pretended to walk the plank, and
soon they were all splashing about, playing and swimming in the
river. They chased each other through the shallow water, and
disappeared along the river and out of sight.

BEARS AHOY!

Now, the three bears left on board the boat did not get on very well together. Oscar was a small, honey-coloured bear. He was good friends with Mabel, who had shaggy brown fur, but neither of them liked Toby. He was bigger than they were and he was a bully. He was always growling at the other bears and telling them what to do.

As soon as the boys were out of sight, Toby leapt to his feet. The boat rocked. Oscar and Mabel begged him to sit down.

"I'm a fearless sailor," cried Toby. "I've sailed the seven seas and now I'm going to sail them again."

Before the others realised what he was doing, Toby had untied the boat, and pushed it away from the bank. The boat lurched from side to side.

"Come on, crew. Look lively!" shouted Toby. "Do as I say or I'll make you walk the plank." Now that it was untied, the little blue boat began to drift out into the river. It turned sideways gently, then caught the main current and began to gather speed.

"Toby!" cried Oscar. "We're moving!"

"Of course we are, you big softie," growled Toby. "We're bold and fearless pirates on the high seas."

Oscar and Mabel clung together in fright, as the little boat sailed down the river, past fields and houses. "Help!" they shouted. "Toby, make it stop!" But Toby was having a great time.

"Ha, ha," shouted Toby. "This is the life!"

Oscar glanced over the side. He wished he hadn't. The sight of everything passing by so quickly made him feel seasick.

"Look out, Toby!" he cried. "We're going to hit the bank. Quickly, steer it away before we crash!"

But Toby did nothing. He simply sat and watched as the little boat careered along, gathering speed as it headed for the bank. Oscar and Mabel clutched the sides of the boat tightly, and clung on fast. They were feeling very frightened. The boat hit the bank with a thump and Toby fell forward. The boat swung round and headed for the middle of the river once more.

"Toby!" shouted Mabel. "Save us!"

But Toby was sitting in the bottom of the boat, rubbing a big bump on his head.

"I can't. I don't know how to sail a boat," he whimpered, feebly. He hid his face in his paws and began to cry. The boat zig-zagged on down the river, with the little bears clinging on to the sides in fright. In time, the river became wider and they could hear the cry of seagulls.

"Oh, Toby," cried Mabel. "We're heading for the sea. Do something!"

"Nobody likes me," wailed Toby. "Now we're going to sink to the bottom of the sea, and you won't like me either!"

Oscar wasn't listening. He had found a rope hanging from the sail. "Let's put the sail up and see if it will blow us to shore," he said.

"We'll be blown out to sea," wailed Toby, but Oscar ignored him, and carried on. The wind filled the sail and the little boat started moving forward. They sailed right across the bay to the far side, and blew up on to the beach.

"Oh, Oscar, you are a hero!" sighed Mabel, hugging him tight. "You saved us!"

Imagine the bears' surprise to see the three little boys running towards them along the beach – they had gone to find the coastguard and raise the alarm. There were hugs and kisses all round when they found the bears safe and sound. And you can be sure that, from that day on, Toby was a much wiser and kinder bear, and he never bullied the others again.

Copycat Max

Max was a little tiger with a bad habit. He was a terrible copycat! He copied everyone and everything. When the parrot said, "Pretty Polly, Pretty Polly," Max repeated it. "Pretty Polly, Pretty Polly!" Then, when the parrot got cross and said, "Shut up, Max, shut up Max," he repeated that as well. It was very annoying.

One day, he set off to explore. "I shall copy everything I see," he said to himself. And that's when the trouble really started!

First, he met a stork standing on one leg.

"Why are you doing that?" asked Max.

"Because it's comfortable," said the stork.

"How long can you do it for?" asked Max.

"For ages!" said the stork. "Only birds can stand like this."

"Hmmm!" said Max, and lifted up one leg.

"Now lift up two more," said the stork. Max did, and fell in a heap on the ground. "Told you!" said the stork. Max picked himself up.

Exploring further, he met a brown chameleon sitting on a green leaf. The amazing thing about chameleons is that they can change colour when they want to. The chameleon saw Max and changed his colour to green, like the leaf! Max could no longer see him.

"Where have you gone?" asked Max, looking everywhere.

"I'm still here," said the chameleon. "Watch this," he added, and he jumped on to a red flower and turned... red!

"Watch this then," said Max, and he lay down on some grass. "Now I'm green," he said.

"You're not," said the chameleon. "Only chameleons can change colour."

"Hmmm!" said Max. He rolled over and over in some mud. "Look," he said, "now I'm brown." Then he rolled in some white feathers. The feathers stuck to the mud. "Look," he said, "now I'm all white!"

"It won't last," said the chameleon.

Max decided to set off for home. He passed the stork still standing on one leg. The stork didn't recognise him.

He arrived home late in the evening. His brothers and sisters were playing down by the river. They saw a white figure coming towards them.

"WOooo!" wailed Max, pretending to be a ghost. "I've come to get you!" The tiger cubs were so scared, they rushed into the river and started to swim to the other side.

"WOooo!" wailed Max and rushed in after them. Of course, as soon as Max got wet, the mud and feathers disappeared. When the others saw it was only Max they were really cross.

"You frightened us," they told him.

"It was only a joke," said Max.

They agreed to forgive him if he promised not to copy anything again.

"Oh, all right," said Max. And, for the moment, he meant it!

Kissable Kitten

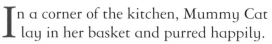

In a corner of the kitchen, Mummy Cat lay in her basket and purred happily. Curled up asleep beside her were four beautiful kittens – a grey kitten called Timmy, a black kitten called Winnie and a stripy kitten called Ginger.

And then there was Kissy, the softest, cutest kitten you ever did see!

Timmy had the biggest blue eyes. They spotted everything. When he and Kissy were in the garden, chasing bumble bees, it was Timmy who spied the water sprinkler.

"Watch out, Kissy!" said Timmy. "You'll get wet!"

"Splish, splash, flipperty-flash!" sang Kissy. "I don't care!" Kissy pushed through the flowers with her little pink nose and shrieked with laughter, as the water sprinkler suddenly covered them both with water.

"Kissy!" spluttered Timmy, shaking water drops from his ears. "Now look what you've done!" But Kissy just rolled around, laughing. "Oh, Timmy," she giggled. "That was so funny!"

KISSABLE KITTEN

"Goodness me," said Mummy Cat, as her kittens dripped water on to the kitchen floor. "Timmy Kitten! You shouldn't have let Kissy get so wet! Now I shall have to dry you both!"

Kissy wriggled and giggled, as Mummy Cat's rough, pink tongue made her wet fur soft and white again. "Sugar and spice, that feels nice!" she sang.

But Timmy wasn't quite so happy. "Ow! Miaow!" he howled, as Mummy Cat's tongue licked him dry.

Kissy loved to explore with Winnie. Winnie had the cutest kitten nose ever and could sniff out all the best yummy food. "Mmm! Smells like jam and cream," said Winnie, her nose and whiskers twitching. Kissy reached up and gently pulled a corner of the tablecloth.

"Mind, Kissy!" said Winnie. "You'll pull everything over!"

"Yum, yum, yum, that cream should be in my tum!" sang Kissy as she pulled the cloth a bit more. Suddenly, the cream jug and jam pot fell to the floor with a crash!

"Oh, Kissy!" shrieked Winnie. "What have you done?"

Jam and cream went everywhere – what a mess! Kissy Kitten could hardly speak for laughing. "Oh, Winnie," she giggled. "That was so funny!"

Mummy Cat threw her paws in the air, when she saw the mess. "Goodness me," she said. "How could you let Kissy get so sticky, Winnie Kitten? Now I shall have to wash you both!"

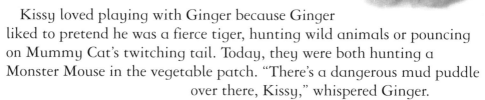

Kissy giggled, as Mummy Cat licked her clean. "Bibble and bat, I like that!" she sang.

But Winnie wasn't happy at all. "Ow! Miaow!" she cried, as Mummy Cat's tongue lapped up the jam.

Kissy loved playing with Ginger because Ginger liked to pretend he was a fierce tiger, hunting wild animals or pouncing on Mummy Cat's twitching tail. Today, they were both hunting a Monster Mouse in the vegetable patch. "There's a dangerous mud puddle over there, Kissy," whispered Ginger. "Whatever you do, don't go in it!"

"Fiddle, fuddle, who cares for a puddle?" sang Kissy as she crawled right through the sticky, squelchy mud. Her beautiful white coat got muddier and muddier. She looked as if she was wearing brown boots!

Ginger hid his eyes. "I can't look!" he said. Kissy laughed and laughed. Then, she shook the mud off her dainty paws – all over Ginger!

Mummy Cat howled when she saw her two dirty kittens. "Ginger Kitten! How could you have let Kissy get so muddy?" she cried. "It will take me ages to clean you both!"

"Piddle and pud, that feels good!" sang Kissy.

Poor Ginger didn't feel good at all. "Ow! Miaow!" he wailed, as Mummy Cat cleaned up his coat.

Mummy Cat looked at her kittens and shook her head. "I just can't understand it," she said. "You've always been such good kittens!" Timmy, Winnie and Ginger all frowned at Kissy, who was fast asleep, purring in their basket.

"It wasn't us!" they cried. "We told Kissy Kitten to be careful! We don't like being bathed!" cried the kittens. "We don't like getting soaked or covered with sticky stuff or coated with mud!"

Mummy Cat looked into the basket. "Kissy?" she said. Kissy opened a bright, green eye and said, "But Mummy, I just love it when you kiss my nose and wash me every time I get messy!"

"What a funny Kissy Kitten you are!" said Mummy Cat, giving her a big lick. "You can have a kiss any time you want. You don't have to get really messy first!"

"No, we'd prefer it if you didn't!" said Timmy.

"But we forgive you," said Winnie and Ginger.

Kissy promised never to get them messy again. Then, they all cuddled up together in their basket and went fast asleep!

King Neptune's Day Off

Trini the little mermaid was happy working in King Neptune's palace. It was beautiful, with fountains and a statue of King Neptune in the courtyard. Trini was happy working there. But some fierce sharks guarded the palace.

On his birthday King Neptune called Trini to see him.

"I'm taking the day off," he said. "I'd like you to organise a birthday banquet for me this evening. So, until then, you will be in charge." And off he went!

The sharks were delighted! They thought they would have some fun while King Neptune was away.

"I'm in charge, so you must do as I say," Trini told them sternly, after the king had left. The sharks just sniggered at her and didn't answer.

Trini set to work. She asked a team of fish to collect shrimps and special juicy seaweed. She told the crabs to collect smooth, pearly shells to use as plates. Then she sent her mermaid friends to collect pieces of coral to decorate the tables.

But the sharks were determined to spoil everything. Soon they saw the fish carrying a net of delicious food. "Give us that," they snapped, and gulped the food down. As soon as the crabs came back with their shell plates, the sharks took the shells and began throwing them to each other.

"Stop it at once!" cried Trini. But the sharks ignored her.

Then the sharks saw the mermaids watching close by. They started to chase them all around the courtyard. "Stop it!" cried Trini. But the sharks just laughed and carried on chasing the mermaids.

Then Trini had an idea. She would trick the sharks! While the sharks were having great fun chasing the mermaids, Trini squeezed through a crack in the hollow statue of King Neptune. The mermaids dropped all their pretty coral and swam away – the sharks couldn't stop laughing. They gathered around King Neptune's statue to plan some more mischief.

Suddenly, a voice like thunder boomed, "Behold, it is I, King Neptune, Emperor of all the Seas and Oceans." The sharks were very frightened. Then the voice bellowed, "Do as Trini commands or you will be banished from the kingdom!"

Then the voice from inside the statue told the sharks to pick up the plates and fetch more food and lay the tables for the banquet. And, while they were busy, Trini crept out from inside the hollow statue where she had been hiding!

So Trini's banquet was a great success. Everyone was there, even the sharks! But they had to stand guard outside the palace, while everyone inside enjoyed themselves. King Neptune had a marvellous time and asked Trini if she would always be his special helper.

"I'd be delighted," she answered, blushing!

Three Little Kittens

Three little kittens they lost their mittens,
    And they began to cry,
Oh, mother dear, we sadly fear
    That we have lost our mittens.

What! lost your mittens, you naughty kittens!
    Then you shall have no pie.
Mee-ow, mee-ow, mee-ow.
    No, you shall have no pie.

The three little kittens they found their mittens,
    And they began to cry,
Oh, mother dear, see here, see here,
    For we have found our mittens.

Put on your mittens, you silly kittens,
    And you shall have some pie.
Purr-r, purr-r, purr-r,
    Oh, let us have some pie.

Gee Up, Neddy

Gee up, Neddy,
    Don't you stop,
Just let your feet go
    Clippety clop.
Clippety clopping,
    Round and round.
Giddy up,
    We're homeward bound.

Slowly, Slowly

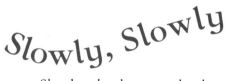

Slowly, slowly, very slowly
    Creeps the garden snail.

Slowly, slowly, very slowly
    Up the garden rail.

Quickly, quickly, very quickly
    Runs the little mouse.

Quickly, quickly, very quickly
    Round about the house.

Hark! Hark!

Hark, hark,
    The dogs do bark,
Beggars are coming to town:
    Some in rags,
    Some in tags,
And some in velvet gowns.

A Cat Came Fiddling

A cat came fiddling out of a barn,
   With a pair of bagpipes under her arm;
She could sing nothing but fiddle cum fee,
   The mouse has married the humble-bee.
Pipe, cat – dance, mouse,
   We'll have a wedding at our good house.

There Was a Little Turtle

There was a little turtle,
   He lived in a box.
He swam in a puddle,
   He climbed on the rocks.

He snapped at a mosquito,
   He snapped at a flea.
He snapped at a minnow,
   He snapped at me.

He caught the mosquito,
   He caught the flea.
He caught the minnow,
   But... he didn't catch me!

The Little Bird

This little bird flaps its wings,
   Flaps its wings,
     flaps its wings,
This little bird flaps its wings,
   And flies away
     in the morning!

As Small as a Mouse

As small as a mouse,
   As wide as a bridge,
As tall as a house,
   As straight as a pin.

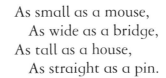

At the Monster Café

Down at the Monster Café there are sights you just would not believe! Monsters love their food, their portions are huge and the colours are scary. As for the ingredients, it might be better not to know, as you will see!

A monster stew is a grisly mixture of turnip tops and vile black drops, and monsters have spaghetti hoops with liquorice loops! They eat brown rats' tails, slugs and snails, and add lots of little flies for decoration.

As for the favourite monster drink – it is lime green, mauve and pink, and made with peas and dead gnat's knees. They say that this goes particularly well with the favourite monster sweets. These are made of dragons' feet, with sugared claws and chocolate paws – sounds really gruesome doesn't it?

Monster snacks start to bubble when you take off the wrapper. They are made from tar and bits of car, which sounds more like torture than a treat! Fortunately most monsters have very large, sharp teeth so they can munch away merrily on their snacks without breaking them.

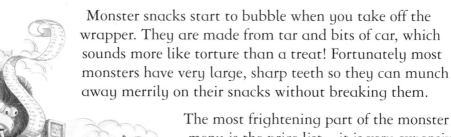

The most frightening part of the monster menu is the price list – it is very expensive to eat at the Monster Café. But to a monster it is a real treat. Will you be saving up for a visit?

Cooking up a Storm

Wizards love to cook. They have a huge cauldron for mixing their magic potions, which means they also have all they need to create huge and wonderful stews for their wizard friends.

There is a difference between what you or I might think of as a stew, and what a stew might be to a wizard. For instance, we can go to a local shop to buy our ingredients whereas a wizard might go down to his local pond! The favourite wizard stew is called Storm and, when you know what goes in it, you will understand why!

First the wizard has to put a handful of cat's whiskers into a cauldron of boiling dirty pond water. Then he adds the tails from three young pups, a big ladle of eyeballs and two cups of froggy slime. This is stirred slowly for seventeen minutes before adding giant fireworks, a bunch of old tin cans, a pair of cymbals and a big bass drum. Then the windows start to shake and the sky darkens – here comes the storm that goes with the stew! As it rains cats and dogs, and a shower of nasty frogs, the stew is ready. The wizard has cooked up a storm!

The Castle in the Clouds

There was once a family that lived in a little house, in a village at the bottom of a mountain. At the top of the mountain was a great, grey castle made of granite. The castle was always shrouded in clouds, so it was known as the castle in the clouds. From the village you could only just see the outline of its high walls and turrets. No one in the village ever went near the castle, for it looked such a gloomy and forbidding place.

Now in this family there were seven children. One by one they went out into the world to seek their fortune, and at last it was the youngest child's turn. His name was Sam. His only possession was a pet cat named Jess, and she was an excellent rat-catcher. Sam was most upset at the thought of leaving Jess behind when he went off to find work, but then he had an idea.

"I'll offer Jess's services at the castle in the clouds. They're bound to need a good ratter, and I'm sure I can find work there, too," he thought.

His parents were dismayed to discover that Sam wanted to find work at the castle, but they could not change his mind. So Sam set off for the castle with Jess at his side. It grew cold and misty as the road wound up the mountainside through thick pine forests. Rounding a bend they suddenly found themselves up against a massive, grey stone wall. They followed the curve of the wall until they came to the castle door.

Sam went up to the door and banged on it. The sound echoed spookily. "Who goes there?" said a voice.

Looking up, Sam saw that a window high in the wall had been opened and a face was eyeing him suspiciously.

"I… I… I wondered if you'd be interested in employing my cat as a rat-catcher," began Sam.

The window slammed shut, but a moment later the castle door opened. Stepping inside, Sam and Jess found themselves face-to-face with an old man. "Rat-catcher, did you say?" said the old man raising one eyebrow. "Very well, but she'd better do a good job or my master will punish us all!"

Sam sent Jess off to prove her worth. Meanwhile Sam asked the old man, who was the castle guard, if there was any work for him, too.

"You can help out in the kitchens, but it's hard work!" the guard said.

Sam was soon working very hard in the kitchens. He spent all day peeling vegetables, cleaning pans and scrubbing the floor.

By midnight he was exhausted. He was about to find a patch of straw to make his bed, when he noticed Jess wasn't around. He set off in search of her down dark passages, up winding staircases, but there was no sign of her. By now he was hopelessly lost but he suddenly saw Jess's green eyes shining like lanterns at the top of a rickety spiral staircase. "Here, Jess!" called Sam softly. But Jess stayed just where she was.

Jess was sitting outside a door and seemed to be listening to something on the other side. Sam put his ear to the door. He could hear the sound of sobbing. He knocked gently at the door. "Who is it?" said a girl's voice.

"I'm Sam, the kitchen boy. Can I come in?" said Sam.

"If only you could," sobbed the voice. "I'm Princess Rose. When my father died my uncle locked me in here so that he could steal the castle. Now I fear I shall never escape!"

Sam pushed and pushed at the door, but to no avail. "Don't worry," he said, "I'll get you out of here."

Sam knew exactly what to do. He had seen a pair of keys hanging on a nail in the rafters high above the guard's head. He had wondered why anyone should put keys out of the reach of any human hand. Now he thought he knew – but first he had to get the keys himself!

When Sam and Jess finally made their way back, they found the guard was fast asleep in his chair right underneath the keys! Jess leaped up on to the shelf behind his head, then she climbed until she reached the rafters. She took the keys in her mouth and carried them down. But, as she jumped from the shelf again, she knocked over a jug and sent it crashing to the floor. The guard woke with a start. "Who goes there?" he growled. He just caught sight of the tip of Jess's tail as she made a dash for the door.

"You go a different way," hissed Sam, running up the stairs to Rose's door, while the old man disappeared off after Jess. Sam put one of the keys in the lock. It fitted! He turned the key and opened the door. There stood the loveliest girl he had ever seen. The princess ran towards him, as he cried, "Quick! There's not a moment to lose." He grabbed her hand and led her out of the tower.

"Give me the keys," she said. She led him down to the castle cellars. At last they came to a tiny door. The princess put the second key in the lock and opened it. Inside was a cupboard, and inside that was a golden casket filled with jewels. "My own casket – stolen by my uncle," cried Rose.

Grabbing the casket the pair ran to the stables and saddled a horse. Suddenly Jess appeared with the guard chasing him. With a mighty leap Jess landed on the back of the horse. "Off we go!" cried Sam.

And that was the last that any of them saw of the castle in the clouds. Sam married the princess and they all lived happily ever after.

The Yellow Bluebells

The fairies at Corner Cottage were always busy. The garden was full of flowers and it was the fairies' job to look after them. You never saw them because they worked at night and hid during the day. Blossom, the youngest fairy, was also one of the busiest. It was her job to paint all the bluebells. Corner Cottage had a lot of bluebells. They spread out under the apple tree like a deep, blue carpet. One evening, Blossom was sick.

"I've got a terrible cold," she told her friend Petal, sniffing loudly. "I don't think I can work tonight."

"I wish I could help," said Petal, "but I've got to spray the flowers with perfume or they won't smell right. You'll have to ask the gnomes."

Oh dear! Nobody liked asking Chip and Chuck, the garden gnomes. All they liked doing was fishing and windsurfing on the pond and playing tricks. Blossom was very worried about asking them.

"No problem!" said Chip and Chuck when she asked them. "Just leave it to us." But when Blossom got up the next morning the gnomes had painted some of the bluebells… YELLOW! She couldn't believe it.

"Have you seen what they've done?" she said to Petal. "What will Jamie think?" Jamie lived in Corner Cottage with his mum and dad, and he played in the garden every day. That morning he came out as usual and made for the apple tree. As he sat on his favourite branch, he looked down. Something looked different.

"I'm sure those flowers were blue," he thought. "Mum," he said, going into the kitchen, "I've picked you some flowers."

"Yellowbells?" said Mum, putting them into a jam jar. "I don't remember planting those."

That night, Blossom was still feeling ill. "You'll have to paint the yellowbells," she told the gnomes, but Chip and Chuck just chuckled.

In the morning, Jamie ran out to the garden and climbed the apple tree. This time the flowers were PINK! He picked a bunch for his mum and she put them in the jam jar with the yellowbells. When Petal told Blossom what had happened, Blossom groaned.

"I just knew something like this would happen." But she was still feeling too sick to work. "Don't worry," said Petal. "Leave it to me." Petal made the naughty gnomes paint all the pinkbells again. And this time she watched them carefully. The gnomes grumbled loudly.

The next morning, all the bluebells were blue again. Blossom was feeling much better. "I'll be glad to get back to work!" she told Petal.

When Jamie and his mum went into the garden, everything was as it should be. The bluebells were the right colour. And there was no sign of the yellowbells or pinkbells.

"It must have been the fairies!" joked Mum.

"Maybe it really was the fairies," thought Jamie as he drifted off to sleep that night.

The Birthday Party

Rosy was walking down the stairs, when the post popped through the letter box and flopped on to the mat. One envelope had a picture of a rabbit and Rosy's name written in big writing on it. She picked it up and rushed into the kitchen. "Look, Mum!" cried Rosy, "a letter for me. Who do you think it's from?"

"I don't know," replied Mum. "Let's open it and find out."

Inside the envelope was an invitation to a party from Rosy's friend, Laura. "Wow! A party!" cried Rosy. "I can't wait!" she said and, with a little bit of help, answered "yes" to the invitation. But then, Rosy began to worry. "What am I going to buy Laura as a present for her birthday?" she asked.

Mum had an idea. "Let's go into town tomorrow and look for something special." So, the next day, Rosy and Mum went to the toy shop. "What does Laura like best?" asked Mum.

"Rabbits," said Rosy. "Laura loves them."

THE BIRTHDAY PARTY

"Come with me," smiled Mum. "I've seen just the thing."

Mum took Rosy to a corner of the toy shop, where they found lots of fluffy toys. And there sat a cute little rabbit, with bright blue trousers and a tiny orange carrot. "Do you think Laura would like that rabbit?" asked Mum.

"She would love him," said Rosy. So, they bought the rabbit and some wrapping paper and went back home.

At home, Rosy wrapped the rabbit in the pretty paper. Then, she drew a card with a big rabbit on the front and wrote her name in red crayon inside it. "Mum," asked Rosy, "what will I do at the party?"

"Well, there will be lots of games to play," said Mum.

"I can't wait!" said Rosy.

At last, the afternoon of the party arrived. Rosy put on her pretty party dress. Mum gave her Laura's card and present. "Mum," asked Rosy, "what if I don't like the food?"

"Don't worry," said Mum. "At parties, there are always lots of tasty things to eat – I promise."

"I can't wait!" cried Rosy and skipped out of the door.

When Rosy arrived at the party, Laura opened the front door. There were lots of children standing behind her, but Rosy couldn't see anyone else that she knew. "Hello, Rosy," said Laura, giving her a big hug. Rosy gave Laura her birthday present. As Laura pulled off the paper, a huge smile spread across her face. "Oh, Rosy!" she cried. "He's perfect!"

Everyone wanted to hold the rabbit. Rosy felt better already. "Time for some games!" called Laura's mum. Rosy stood by the door and watched.

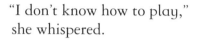

"I don't know how to play," she whispered.

"Just do what I do," said Laura and held her friend's hands. Rosy was soon having a wonderful time. Party games were great fun.

Just then, Laura's mum said, "It's time for the birthday tea."

Rosy couldn't wait to see what there was to eat. She was feeling really hungry! "Wow!" gasped Rosy, when she saw the party food. All of her favourite things were there – sausages, pizza, cakes and strawberry jelly! There were balloons, paper plates and cups, which all had rabbits on them.

Rosy sat next to Laura. "Wait till you see my cake," laughed her friend. At that moment, Laura's mum walked into the room. She was carrying a birthday cake – in the shape of a big rabbit! Laura blew out the candles and everyone sang "Happy birthday!" as loudly as they could.

THE BIRTHDAY PARTY

After tea, everyone played Pass the Parcel. Rosy really liked this game. It was very exciting, waiting for the music to stop and then watching, while someone tore the paper off the parcel. "I can't wait for my turn," thought Rosy. Suddenly, the music did stop, just as Rosy held the parcel. And this time, there was only one piece of paper left. She ripped it off – inside was a jigsaw puzzle.

It wasn't long before mums and dads came to take their children home. "Thanks for my rabbit," said Laura, to Rosy.

"And thanks for a great party," said Rosy. Then, Laura gave everyone a balloon and a badge – with a rabbit on it. On the way home, Mum asked Rosy if she'd had a good time.

"Oh, yes!" said Rosy. "The games were fun, Laura's other friends were great and the food was really yummy! Mum," asked Rosy, "how long is it until my birthday?"

"About four weeks," said Mum. "Why?"

"Please can I have a party?" replied Rosy.

"I've got lots of friends to invite and I know just which games I want to play. And I'd really like a big dinosaur cake."

"I can't wait!" laughed Mum.

The Mermaid in the Pool

John and Julia were on holiday at the seaside. Their mum and dad had found an amazing house with a big swimming pool. But, best of all, their bedroom overlooked the beach. It was perfect!

The first night there was a storm. The wind howled and waves crashed over the beach, right up to the house. The children sat on the bed watching the storm outside.

In the morning, the garden furniture had blown over, there was seaweed all over the lawn and there was a mermaid swimming up and down the swimming pool! John and Julia rushed outside but, when the mermaid saw them coming, she huddled in a corner of the pool. "I'm sorry I swam into your blue pool," said the frightened mermaid.

"It's okay!" said Julia gently. "We didn't mean to frighten you. We just wanted to meet you. We've never seen a mermaid before."

"My name is Marina," said the mermaid. "I was playing in the sea with my friend Blue the dolphin, when the storm began. A huge wave washed me in, and now I'm stranded, and Blue is missing!"

"We'll help you look for Blue," said Julia at once. "We might be able to see your friend from our bedroom window."

When their mum and dad were safely out of the way, John and Julia found a wheelbarrow and wheeled Marina into the house. "I've only had sky over my head," said Marina. "The house won't fall down will it?"

"Of course not," smiled John. They showed Marina all sorts of things she had never seen before. She thought the moving pictures on the television were weird. She thought Julia's teddy bear was wonderful, and that beds were the silliest things she had ever seen! But, although they looked out of the window, there was no sign of Blue the dolphin in the sea.

"I have to go home soon!" Marina said sadly. "I can't stay out of the water for long, and I must find Blue. If only I hadn't lost my shell horn in the storm I could call him."

"We'll take you down to the sea," said John. "And help you look for your shell," said Julia.

They lifted Marina back into the wheelbarrow and pushed her down to the beach. They spent the rest of the day searching for Marina's shell along the seashore. Suddenly, Julia spotted a large shell half buried in the sand. John found a stick and dug it out.

"It's my shell!" cried Marina. They washed off the sand and Marina blew into it. The most beautiful sound drifted out across the waves and, straight away, there was an answering call! Far out to sea, they saw a streak of blue-grey leaping high over the waves, swimming towards them. It was Blue the dolphin!

Marina gave a cry of joy and swam to meet him. She flung her arms round his neck and hugged him. Then she called out to the watching children. "Thank you both for helping me."

"See you next year!" called John and Julia.

And they watched as Marina and Blue swam swiftly and smoothly together, back out to sea.

The Owl and the Pussycat

The Owl and the Pussycat went to sea
  In a beautiful pea-green boat,
They took some honey, and plenty of money,
  Wrapped up in a five-pound note.

The Owl looked up to the stars above,
  And sang to a small guitar,
"O lovely Pussy! O Pussy, my love,
  What a beautiful Pussy you are,
You are, you are!
What a beautiful Pussy you are!"

I Saw Three Ships

I saw three ships come sailing by,
  Come sailing by, come sailing by;
I saw three ships come sailing by,
  On New Year's Day in the morning.

And what do you think was in them then,
  Was in them then, was in them then?
And what do you think was in them then,
  On New Year's Day in the morning?

Three pretty girls were in them then,
  Were in them then, were in them then;
Three pretty girls were in them then,
  On New Year's Day in the morning.

And one could whistle, and one could sing,
  And one could play on the violin –
Such joy there was at my wedding,
  On New Year's Day in the morning.

Bobbie Shaftoe's Gone to Sea

Bobbie Shaftoe's gone to sea,
  Silver buckles at his knee;
When he comes back
He'll marry me,
  Bonny Bobbie Shaftoe!

If All the Seas Were One Sea

If all the seas were one sea,
　　What a great sea that would be!
And if all the trees were one tree,
　　What a great tree that would be!
And if all the axes were one axe,
　　What a great axe that would be!

And if all the men were one man,
　　What a great man he would be!
And if the great man took the great axe,
　　And cut down the great tree,
And let it fall into the great sea,
　　What a splish splash that would be!

I Saw a Ship a-Sailing

I saw a ship a-sailing,
　　A-sailing on the sea;
And, oh! it was all laden
　　With pretty things for thee!

There were comfits in the cabin,
　　And apples in the hold
The sails were made of silk,
　　And the masts were made of gold.

The four-and-twenty sailors
　　That stood between the decks,
Were four-and-twenty white mice
　　With chains about their necks.

The captain was a duck,
　　With a packet on his back;
And when the ship began to move,
　　The captain said, "Quack! quack!"

Dance to Your Daddy

Dance to your daddy,
　　My little babby;
Dance to your daddy,
　　My little lamb.

You shall have a fishy,
　　In a little dishy;
You shall have a fishy
　　When the boat comes in.

Shanty Goes to Sea

Shanty, the harbour kitten, just loved fish. He ate every scrap that the fishermen threw away. And sometimes, when nobody was looking, he even helped himself to a few whole fish that should have gone to market.

"Don't you ever get tired of fish?" asked his friend Gull. But Shanty just shook his head and continued nibbling on a tasty sardine. He just couldn't get enough fish!

One day, Shanty had a brilliant idea. "There's only one thing that would be better than being a harbour kitten," he told Gull. "And that would be being a boat kitten. Then I could eat all the fish I wanted."

So the next morning, when none of the fishermen were looking, Shanty crept aboard the *Salty Sardine*, the biggest of all the fishing boats in the harbour. Everybody was so busy that they didn't notice the stowaway hidden beneath an old raincoat.

The sea was calm as the boat chugged out to sea, and Shanty had a great time dreaming about all the fish that he was going to eat.

When the fishermen started pulling in the nets, Shanty couldn't believe his eyes. He was in kitten heaven. He'd never seen so many fish. There were mackerel. There were cod. There were haddock. And there were Shanty's favourite, sardines.

There were so many that nobody noticed when a few began to disappear under the old raincoat.

Shanty ate and ate, until he could eat no more. Then he curled up and settled down to sleep. But, just as he was dozing off, something strange began to happen.

The *Salty Sardine* began to creak and moan. Then it began to sway and rock. Water sprayed over the sides as it bounced over the waves then crashed back down again. Shanty's head began to reel and his

stomach began to roll. Oh, how he wished he hadn't eaten so many fish! Oh, how he wished he'd stayed on dry land!

"We're going to drown," wailed Shanty, as a big wave crashed over the raincoat.

Soaked right through, Shanty peered out to see what the fishermen were doing. He couldn't believe his eyes. Instead of running about and screaming, they were carrying on with their work. One of them, who Shanty thought must be the captain, was even whistling. And another was eating a sausage roll. It seemed that for them, this was a normal day's work.

When the *Salty Sardine* finally got back to the harbour, Shanty couldn't get off fast enough.

"How is life as a boat kitten?" asked Gull, when he came visiting later that evening.

"Ah!" said Shanty, after he'd finished nibbling on a scrap of sardine. "Boats are all very well but give me the harbour any day. After all, how many fish can one kitten eat!"

Granny Casts a Spell

Susie was very fond of her Granny. Each day, when Susie got home from school, Granny was always there, sitting by the fire, knitting. Granny knitted so fast that sometimes it seemed as though the knitting needles sparked in the firelight.

"Do you know," Granny would say, "that I'm really a witch?" Susie always laughed when Granny said that because she didn't look at all like a witch. She had a smiling face and kind eyes and she never wore black. Not ever. When Granny wasn't looking, Susie would take a peek inside her wardrobe just in case she might find a broomstick or a witch's hat. But she never found so much as a book of spells.

"I don't believe you're a witch," said Susie.

"I am," replied Granny, "and I'll cast a spell one day. You'll know when that day comes, for my needles will start to knit by themselves."

After that, Susie kept a careful watch over Granny's needles, but they always lay quite still in the basket of knitting.

One day, Susie was playing in her garden when she heard the sound of weeping. The sound seemed to be coming from under the old tree in the corner.

She walked towards
the tree and as she
did so the crying
noise got
louder, but
she could not
see anyone
there. Then
she looked down
at her feet and there

– sitting on a mossy stone – was a tiny little man. He was neatly dressed
in a yellow velvet waistcoat and knickerbockers. On his feet were
beautiful, shiny, buckled shoes, and a three-cornered hat with a wren's
feather in it trembled on his shaking head. When the little man saw
Susie, he stopped crying and started to dab his eyes with a fine lace
handkerchief.

"Whatever can the matter be?" asked Susie, crouching down.

"Oh dear, oh dear!" sobbed the little man. "I am the fairy princess's
tailor and she has asked me to make her a lovely gown to wear to the
May Ball tonight, but a wicked elf has played a trick on me and turned
all my fine gossamer fabric into bats' wings. Now I shall never be able
to make the princess's gown and she will be very angry with me."
He started to cry again.

"Don't cry!" said Susie. "I'm sure I can help. My Granny's got a
sewing basket full of odds and ends. I'll see if she's got anything nice for
a party dress. I'm sure she won't mind sparing some – after all, you
won't need much," she said. At that, the little man looked a bit more
cheerful.

"Wait here," said Susie, "while I run indoors and see." She ran up the
garden path and in through the back door.

"Granny, Granny!" she called. She ran into the sitting room expecting to find Granny knitting by the fire. But Granny had her eyes closed and she was whispering to herself. On her lap was her knitting – and the needles were moving all by themselves, so that the yarn danced up and down on the old lady's knees.

At first Susie was too astounded to move. Then she thought, "I hope Granny's not casting a bad spell. I must see if the little tailor is alright."

She ran back down the garden path and there sat the tailor, surrounded by a great pile of gorgeous gossamer, shining in the sunlight.

"I've never seen such fine material – ever!" he exclaimed. "But where did it come from? I just closed my eyes to dab them with my hanky and when I opened them again – there it was!"

"I don't know," said Susie, "but I think my Granny might have had something to do with it."

"Well, I'd never be able to thank her enough," said the tailor. "I shall be able to make the finest gown in the whole of fairyland. The princess will dance all night in the prettiest dress there ever was. I'm also indebted to you, for it was you who helped me in the first place. I would like it very much if you came to the May Ball, too."

"Why, thank you so much," Susie replied, "I should like that very much." She didn't want to hurt the tailor's feelings but she knew she couldn't go – she was far too big to go to a fairy ball!

"Well, I must get on with the dress now," said the little man, reaching for a pair of fairy scissors. "See you tonight!" And with that he vanished.

That night, Susie wondered if the fairies really were having a ball. How she longed to be there! Once she thought she heard a tapping at the window. Was that the fairy tailor she saw through the glass — or was she imagining it? In the middle of the night she awoke with a start. There was a click, clicking noise at the end of her bed.

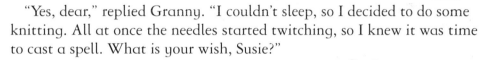

"Granny is that you?" asked Susie.

"Yes, dear," replied Granny. "I couldn't sleep, so I decided to do some knitting. All at once the needles started twitching, so I knew it was time to cast a spell. What is your wish, Susie?"

"I... I..." stammered Susie, "I want to go to the May Ball," she blurted.

"Then you shall, my dear," said Granny.

In an instant, Susie felt herself shrinking and when she looked down she saw she was wearing a beautiful gown and tiny satin slippers. Then she floated on gossamer wings out through the window and off to the Ball.

The next morning, Susie woke up in her bed. Had it all been a dream – the revelry, the fairy food, the frog band, the dance with the fairy prince? Then she saw something peeping out from under her pillow. And what do you think it was? It was a tiny, tiny shred of the finest gossamer fabric.

A Thorn

I went to the wood and got it;
   I sat me down and looked at it;
The more I looked at it the less I liked it;
   And I brought it home because I couldn't help it.

I Met a Man

As I was going up the stair
   I met a man who wasn't there.
He wasn't there again today –
   Oh! how I wish he'd go away!

Cross Patch

Cross patch,
Draw the latch,
Sit by the fire and spin;
   Take a cup,
   And drink it up,
Then call your neighbours in.

Teeth

Thirty white horses upon a red hill,
   Now they tramp, now they champ,
Now they all stand still.

Dreams

Here we are all, by day;
   by night we are hurled
By dreams, each one into
   a several world.

A Star

I have a little sister, they call her Peep, Peep;
   She wades the waters deep, deep, deep;
She climbs the mountains high, high, high;
   Poor little creature she has but one eye.

Silly Sally

Silly Sally swiftly shooed
　　seven silly sheep.
The seven silly sheep
　　Silly Sally shooed shilly-shallied south.
These sheep shouldn't sleep in a shack;
　　sheep should sleep in a shed.

My Mother and Your Mother

My mother and your mother
　　Went over the way;
Said my mother to your mother,
　　It's chop-a-nose day!

I Went Up One Pair of Stairs

I went up one pair of stairs.
　　Just like me.
I went up two pair of stairs.
　　Just like me.
I went into a room.
　　Just like me.
I looked out of a window.
　　Just like me.
And there I saw a monkey.
　　Just like me.

I am a Gold Lock

I am a gold lock.
　　I am a gold key.
I am a silver lock.
　　I am a silver key.
I am a brass lock.
　　I am a brass key.
I am a lead lock.
　　I am a lead key.
I am a monk lock.
　　I am a monk key!

Teddy Bear Tears

"**B**oo hoo! I want to go home!"
As a little fairy called Mavis flew past the rubbish dump, holding her nose, she heard an unmistakable sound coming from the other side of a very smelly pile of rubbish.

"Oh dear. Those sound like teddy bear tears," she said to herself. "I'd better go and see if I can help."

She flew down to take a look, and, sure enough, there amongst a heap of old potato peelings and banana skins sat a very old, very sad teddy indeed. Mavis sat and held his paw, while he told her tearfully what had happened:

"My owner, Matilda, was told to clean out her room. She's terribly messy, but she's sweet and kind," Teddy sniffed. "She threw me out with an old blanket by mistake – she didn't realise I was tucked up having a sleep inside it. Then some men in a big, dirty truck came and emptied me out of the dustbin and brought me here. But I want to go home!" And with that poor Teddy started to cry again.

"There, there," said Mavis. "I'll help to get you home. But first I'll need two teddy bear tears." She unscrewed the lid of a little jar, and scooped two big salty tears into it from Teddy's cheeks.

"What do you need those for?" asked Teddy, feeling rather bewildered.

"Just a little fairy magic!" said Mavis. "Now wait here, and I promise I'll be back soon." And with a wave of her wand, she disappeared.

Teddy pulled the blanket around him, and sat trying to be brave, and not to cry. He stayed like that all night, feeling cold and alone and frightened. How he wished he was back in his warm, cosy home.

Meanwhile Mavis was very busy. She flew back and forth around the neighbourhood, until she heard the sound of sobbing coming from an open

window. She flew down onto the windowsill and peered inside. A little girl was lying on the bed, with her mummy sitting beside her.

"I want my teddy!" she cried.

"Well if you weren't so messy, Matilda, you wouldn't lose things," said Mummy gently.

"But I cleaned my room today!" said Matilda.

"Well, try and go to sleep now," said Mummy, kissing her goodnight, "and we'll look for Teddy in the morning."

Mavis watched as poor Matilda lay sobbing into her pillow, until at last she fell fast asleep. Then Mavis flew down from the windowsill, took out the little jar, and rubbed Teddy's tears onto Matilda's sleeping eyes. With a little fizzle of stars, the fairy magic began to work, and Matilda started to dream. She could see an old tyre, a newspaper, some tin cans, some orange peel, a blanket... wait a minute, it was her blanket, and there, wrapped inside it was her teddy, with a big tear running down his cheek! Teddy was at the rubbish dump!

The next morning, Matilda woke with a start, and remembered her dream at once. She ran downstairs to the kitchen, where Mummy was making breakfast, and told her all about it.

"We have to go to the rubbish dump! We have to save Teddy!" said Matilda.

Mummy tried to explain that it was just a dream, but Matilda wouldn't listen, she was sure she was right. So in the end they set off to take a look.

They arrived just as a big machine was scooping up the rubbish and heading for the

crusher. And there, on top of the scoop, clinging to the edge, was Teddy!

Mavis appeared, hovering in the air above him.

"Don't worry, we'll save you!" she said. She waved her wand in a bright flash above Teddy. Matilda looked up and spotted him at once.

"There he is!" she cried, pointing frantically at Teddy. "He's going to be squashed! Mummy, do something, quick!" Mummy ran up to the man driving the machine, waving her arms in the air.

He stopped his machine just in time.

Soon Teddy and Matilda were reunited, and there were more tears, although this time they were happy ones. And from then on, Matilda's room was the tidiest room you have ever seen.

Just As Well, Really!

Rumpus liked water. He liked the drippiness and droppiness, the splashiness and sloppiness of it!

He liked it so much that, whenever there was water around, Rumpus somehow always managed to fall into it!

But Mum loved Rumpus, so every time she simply sighed and she mopped up the mess.

Rumpus loved mud. He loved the way you could plodge in it, splodge in it, slide in it and glide in it!

Rumpus somehow always managed to get covered in it!

But Dad loved Rumpus, so every time he simply sighed and he sponged off the splatters.

Rumpus enjoyed paint. He liked to splatter and dash it, to spread and

346

splash it! Rumpus somehow managed to get it everywhere!

But Rumpus' brother loved him, so every time he simply sighed and cleaned himself up.

Rumpus liked to find out how things worked. He loved the prodding and probing, the wiggling and the jiggling, the unscrewing and the undoing!

He loved it so much that, whenever Rumpus was around, things didn't work for long!

But Granny loved Rumpus, so she simply sighed and she tidied away the clutter.

Rumpus loved his mum, dad, brother and granny. Rumpus' mum, dad, brother and granny loved Rumpus... just as well, really!

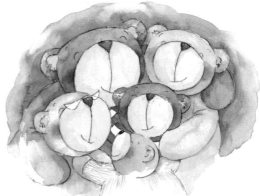

I Love Little Pussy

I love little pussy, her coat is so warm;
And if I don't hurt her she'll do me no harm.
So I'll not pull her tail nor drive her away,
But pussy and I very gently will play.

Pussycat Mole

Pussycat Mole,
Jumped over a coal,
And in her best petticoat
burnt a great hole.
Poor pussy's weeping,
she'll have no more milk,
Until her best petticoat's
mended with silk.

Pussycat, Pussycat

Pussycat, pussycat, where
have you been?
I've been to London to visit
the Queen.
Pussycat, pussycat, what
did you there?
I frightened a little mouse
under her chair.

Pussycat Sits by the Fire

Pussycat sits by the fire.
How did she come there?
In walks the little dog,
Says, "Pussy! are you there?
How do you do, Mistress Pussy?
Mistress Pussy, how d'ye do?"
"I thank you kindly, little dog,
I fare as well as you!"

Mary Had a Little Lamb

Mary had a little lamb,
   Its fleece was white as snow,
And everywhere that Mary went
   The lamb was sure to go.

It followed her to school one day,
   Which was against the rule;
It made the children laugh and play
   To see a lamb in school.

Frisky Lamb

A frisky lamb
   And a frisky child
Playing their pranks
   In a cowslip meadow:
The sky all blue
   And the air all mild
And the fields all sun
   And the lanes half-shadow.

Baa, Baa, Black Sheep

Baa, baa, black sheep, have you any wool?
   Yes, sir, yes, sir, three bags full;
One for the master, one for the dame,
   And one for the little boy that lives down the lane.

On the Grassy Banks

On the grassy banks
   Lambkins at their pranks;
Woolly sisters, woolly brothers,
   Jumping off their feet,
While their woolly mothers
   Watch them and bleat.

Sleeping Beauty

Once upon a time, in a land far, far away, there lived a king and queen who were kind and good. When the queen gave birth to a baby girl, the whole kingdom rejoiced.

When it was time for the baby to be christened, the king and queen arranged a great celebration. They asked the seven good fairies of the kingdom to be the baby's godmothers. But, to their surprise, eight fairies arrived at the feast.

The eighth fairy was ugly and old, and no one had seen her for years. The king and queen, thinking she was dead, hadn't invited her to take part in the ceremony.

Soon it was time for the fairies to give the baby princess their magical presents. The first gave her the gift of beauty, the second gave her wisdom. The third fairy said she would be graceful, the fourth said that she would dance like the wind. The fifth and sixth gave her the gifts of music and song, so that she would sing and play like an angel.

Just before the seventh fairy stepped up to give the princess her gift, the eighth fairy pushed ahead of her. "The princess," she cackled, "will prick her finger on the spindle of a spinning wheel – and die!"

Everyone in the room was horrified, and the queen began to cry. But then the seventh fairy stepped forward. "Here is my gift," she said. "The princess will not die. Instead, when she pricks her finger, she will fall asleep for a hundred years. At the end of that time, a prince will come to wake her up."

The king and queen were relieved, but even so they ordered every spinning wheel in the kingdom to be destroyed. They couldn't bear to think of anything hurting their daughter.

The years passed and the princess grew into a lovely young girl, as wise, beautiful and graceful as the fairies had promised.

On the day of her sixteenth birthday, she was wandering through the castle when she came to a small room in a tall tower. Inside, an old woman sat spinning thread.

"My dear," cackled the old woman, "come here and try this for yourself."

As soon as the princess's hand touched the spindle, she pricked her finger and fell to the floor in a deep sleep.

When they discovered their daughter, the king and queen were heartbroken, for they knew that she would not wake for a hundred years. They called for the palace guards, who gently laid the sleeping princess on a golden stretcher and carried her to the royal bedchamber. There they placed her on a bed with silken pillows and velvet covers. The king and queen watched over her and cried.

"Oh, my dear," said the queen to her husband. "How are we ever going to cope without our darling daughter?"

The fairy who had saved the princess's life heard what had happened. Worried that the princess would wake up in a world where she knew no one, she cast a spell over the whole castle. Everyone, from the guards and the kitchen maids to the gardeners and the cooks — even the princess's pet dog — fell into a deep, deep sleep.

Then the fairy made tall trees and twisting, sharp brambles grow around the castle, surrounding it with a thick thorny wall that no one could get through. Only the very tops of the castle's towers could be seen.

And so a hundred years went by.

One day, a prince from a nearby land was out riding when he saw the tops of the castle towers rising from the middle of the thick, dark wood. He asked some of the country people about it, and they told him the story of the Sleeping Beauty.

"Many people have wanted to get through those thorns," they told him, "but they have all died trying."

The prince was determined to be the one who succeeded and set off towards the mysterious castle. To the prince's amazement, the thorny brambles and the twisting branches of the dark trees let him pass through easily.

He reached the castle door, and went inside.

The prince walked through many halls and chambers where people and animals slept as if they were dead. He searched every room and chamber, until he found the very one where the beautiful princess slept.

"Oh, princess!" cried the prince. "You are more beautiful than the most delicate rose ever found."

The prince moved quietly towards the sleeping princess and gazed down lovingly at her. He gently took her tiny hand in his, and as love filled his heart, he knelt beside her and slowly kissed her red lips. Instantly the princess's eyes opened.

"Is it you, my prince?" she said, when she saw him. "I have waited such a long time for you!"

At that moment the spell was broken, and everyone else in the castle woke up, too.

That evening, the princess's sixteenth birthday was celebrated with a joyous party – just a hundred years too late!

The princess and her prince danced together all evening, and, soon after, they were married. They lived together in happiness for many, many years.

The Mermaid Fair

Jason loved diving and he was very good at it. He loved to dive for shellfish and sponges, but mainly he loved to look for pearls. Pearls are jewels of the sea and he collected even the tiniest one.

One day Jason was diving when he saw a sign on a rock. Jason was very surprised. He swam closer and was even more surprised to read the words: MERMAID FAIR TODAY!

Jason had heard of mermaids, of course, but he'd never seen one! Jason took a huge gulp of air and swam towards the fair. He hid behind a rock and watched. There was a crowd of mermaids at the fair, some were riding dolphins, some were swimming in races and some were playing games at the stalls. And there were pearls! There were stalls where you could win a pearl by throwing a hoop over it. Another where, if you pulled down a lever and saw three shells in a row, a hundred white pearls came out of a hole at the bottom! Two of the mermaids noticed Jason watching and came over to him.

"You're a strange sort of fish!" teased the fair-haired mermaid.

"I think it must be a boy!" laughed the dark-haired mermaid.

"Hello," said Jason. To Jason's amazement, he found he could talk and breathe under water! "Can I take part in your fair? I'd love to win some pearls!"

"Oh, you don't want dull old pearls," said one. "What you want are these," and showed Jason a plastic comb with a flower on it. The mermaid had found it one day in a rock pool and thought it was the most beautiful thing she'd ever seen. Jason told her he would bring her many combs if she would show him how to win a pearl.

"That's easy!" she told him. "You just have to win the dolphin race!" So Jason entered the dolphin race. But it was not as easy as he thought. He found that dolphins are very slippery to ride, and jumping through a hoop underwater is impossible. Unless, of course, you are a mermaid!

It was nearly time to go and Jason had not won a single prize! At the very last stall there was the biggest pearl he had ever seen – almost as big as a coconut. He had to throw a sponge at the pearl to knock it over. If there was one thing Jason could do, it was throw a sponge.

The mermaids gathered round to cheer him on. He had one or two near misses and then, amidst lots of laughter, he knocked the huge pearl off the stand with his third try.

"You've won!" the mermaids shouted excitedly. "The pearl is yours!"

Jason swam back to his boat, delighted. The next day he returned clutching a box filled with pretty plastic combs. When the mermaids saw them they danced for joy in the waves and kissed him on both cheeks.

After that Jason saw the mermaids whenever he went diving, and he always took them a special plastic comb.

Mrs Mouse's Holiday

Mrs Mouse was very excited. All year she had been so busy. First there had been nuts and berries to gather in readiness for winter. Then she had needed to give her little house a big spring clean to make it nice and fresh. Now, as the warm sun shone down on the trees and flowers of her woodland home, she had promised herself a well-deserved holiday. But getting ready for holidays seemed to make one busier than ever! There was so much to do!

First she took out her little case, opened it and placed it carefully on her neatly made bed. Then she rushed to her cupboard and selected some fine holiday dresses. Back to her case she scuttled and laid them in. Now she chose several pairs of shoes – a nice pair of sandals for walking along the front in, a pair of smart shoes for shopping in, an even smarter pair for going to dinner in, and another pair just in case!

"I'll need a couple of sun hats," she thought to herself, and so into the case they went as well. These were followed by a coat, some gloves and a scarf (just in case the breeze got up and it became cold). Then, in case it became very sunny, in went some sunglasses, some sun cream and a sunshade. But, oh dear, there were so many things in the case that it refused to shut. She tried sitting on it, and bouncing on it, but still it stubbornly would not close.

So out from the case came all the things that she had just put in, and Mrs Mouse scurried to the cupboard again and chose an even bigger case. This time they all fitted perfectly, and she shut the case with a big sigh of relief.

Now she was ready to go to the seaside for her holiday. She sat on the train, with her case on the rack above her head, munching her hazelnut sandwiches and looking eagerly out of the window hoping to see the sea. Finally, as the train chuffed around a bend, there it was! A great, deep blue sea shimmering in the sun, with white gulls soaring over the cliffs and headlands.

"I'm really looking forward to a nice, quiet rest," she said to herself.

Her guesthouse was very comfortable, and so close to the sea that she could smell the clean, salty air whenever she opened her window. "This is the life," she thought. "Nice and peaceful."

After she had put her clothes away, she put on her little swimming costume and her sun hat and packed her beach bag. Now she was ready for some peaceful sunbathing!

At the beach, she found herself a quiet spot, closed her eyes and was soon fast asleep. But not for long! A family of voles had arrived on the beach, and they weren't trying to have a quiet time at all. The youngsters in the family yelled at the top of their voices, splashed water everywhere, and sent their beach ball tumbling all over Mrs Mouse's neatly laid out beach towel.

Just as Mrs Mouse thought that it couldn't get any noisier, along came a crowd of ferrets. Now if you've ever sat on a beach next to a crowd of ferrets, you'll know what it's like. Their noisy shouting and singing made Mrs Mouse's head buzz.

Mrs Mouse couldn't stand it a moment longer. She was just wondering where she might find some peace and quiet when she spotted a rock just a little way out to sea.

"If I swim out to that rock," she thought, "I will surely have some peace and quiet there." She gathered up her belongings and swam over to the rock. It was a bit lumpy, but at least it was quiet. Soon she was fast asleep again.

Just then the rock started to move slowly out to sea! It wasn't really a rock at all, you see, but a turtle which had been dozing near the surface. Off into the sunset it went, with Mrs Mouse dozing on its back, quite unaware of what was happening.

Eventually, the turtle came to a deserted island. At that moment, Mrs Mouse woke up. She looked at the empty beach, and, without even knowing she had been sleeping on a turtle, she jumped off and swam to the shore, thinking it was the beach that she had just left.

Just then, the turtle swam off, and Mrs Mouse suddenly realised what had happened. For a moment she was horrified. But then she looked at the quiet, palm-fringed beach with no one about but herself, and thought of the noisy beach she had just left.

"Well, perhaps this isn't such a bad place to spend a quiet holiday after all," she thought.

And that's just what she did. Day after day she lazed on her own private beach with no one to disturb her. There were plenty of coconuts and fruits to eat, and she wanted for nothing. She even made herself a cosy bed from palm leaves.

Eventually, though, she started to miss her own little house in the woods and decided it was time to get back home. First she took half a coconut and nibbled out the tasty inside. "That will make a fine boat to sit in," she said.

Next she found a palm leaf and stuck it in the bottom of the shell. She took her little boat to the water's edge and, as the wind caught her palm leaf sail, off she floated back to the boarding house to get her belongings. As she sailed slowly back she thought, "This is the quietest holiday I've ever had. I may come back here next year!"

Like a Duck to Water

Mrs Duck swam proudly across the farm pond followed by a line of fluffy ducklings. Hidden in the safety of the nest, Dozy Duckling peeked out and watched them go. He wished he was brave enough to go with them but he was afraid of the water! Instead, he pretended to be asleep, and Mrs Duck told the others to leave him alone.

When they returned that night they told him tales of all the scary animals they had met by the pond.

"There's a big thing with hot breath called Horse," said Dotty.

"There's a huge smelly pink thing called Pig," said Dickie.

"But worst of all," said Doris, "there's a great grey bird, called Heron. Pig says he gobbles up little ducklings for breakfast!"

At that all the little ducklings squawked with fear and excitement.

Next morning, Mrs Duck hurried the ducklings out for their morning parade. Dozy kept his eyes shut until they had gone, then looked up to see a great grey bird towering over him! He leapt into the water crying, "Help, wait for me!" But the others started laughing!

"It's a trick! Heron won't eat you. We just wanted you to come swimming. And you've taken to it like a duck to water!"

In the Tree-top

"Rock-a-by, baby, up in the tree-top!"
Mother his blanket is spinning;
And a light little rustle
that never will stop,

Breezes and boughs are beginning.
Rock-a-by, baby, swinging so high!
Rock-a-by!

"When the wind blows,
then the cradle will rock."
Hush! now it stirs in the bushes;
Now with a whisper, a flutter of talk,
Baby and hammock it pushes.
Rock-a-by, baby! shut, pretty eye!
Rock-a-by!

The Song of the Stars

We are the stars which sing,
We sing with our light.
We are the birds of fire
We fly over the sky,
Our light is a voice.
We make a road for spirits,
For the spirits to pass over.
Among us are three hunters
Who chase a bear;
There never was a time
When they were not hunting.
We look down on
the mountains.
This is the song of the stars.

Hush, Little Baby

Hush, little baby, don't say a word,
Papa's going to buy you a mocking bird.
If the mocking bird won't sing,
Papa's going to buy you a diamond ring.
If the diamond ring turn to brass,
Papa's going to buy you a looking-glass.
If the looking-glass gets broke,
Papa's going to buy you a billy-goat.
If that billy-goat runs away,
Papa's going to buy you another today.

Humpty Dumpty's Poem

In winter, when the fields are white,
   I sing this song for your delight –
In spring, when woods are getting green,
   I'll try and tell you what I mean.
In summer, when the days are long,
   Perhaps you'll understand the song:
In autumn, when the leaves are brown,
   Take pen and ink, and write it down.

I sent a message to the fish:
   I told them "This is what I wish."
The little fishes of the sea,
   They sent an answer back to me.
The little fishes' answer was
   "We cannot do it, Sir, because –"
I sent to them again to say
   "It will be better to obey."

A Cradle Song

Golden slumbers kiss your eyes,
   Smiles awake you when you rise.
Sleep, pretty wantons, do not cry,
   And I will sing a lullaby:
Rock them, rock them, lullaby.

Care is heavy, therefore sleep you;
   You are care, and care must
     keep you.
Sleep, pretty wantons, do not cry,
   And I will sing a lullaby:
Rock them, rock them, lullaby.

Frog Went a-Courtin'

Mr Froggie went a-courtin' an' he did ride;
   Sword and pistol by his side.
He went to Missus Mousie's hall,
   Gave a loud knock and gave a loud call.

"Pray, Missus Mousie, air you within?"
   "Yes, kind sir, I set an' spin."
He tuk Miss Mousie on his knee,
   An' sez, "Miss Mousie, will ya marry me?"

The Cow who Jumped over the Moon

Boing, boing, boing! Bouncy Bunny kicked up her heels and bounded happily across the field.

"I can bounce high in the air, watch me!" she called to the other animals on the farm. Her fluffy white tail bobbed up and down.

"Very good!" said Silly Sheep, who was easily impressed.

"Yes, very good," said Swift, the sheepdog. "But not as good as me. I can jump right over the gate." With that, he leapt over the gate and into the field.

"Amazing!" said Silly Sheep.

"Yes, amazing," said Harry Horse, with a flick of his mane. "But not as amazing as me. I can jump right over that hedge. Watch me!" And with that, he galloped around the field, then  leapt high into the air, and sailed over the tall hedge.

"Unbelievable!" said Silly Sheep.

"Yes, unbelievable," said Daisy, the cow, chewing lazily on a clump of grass. "But not as unbelievable as me. I can jump right over the moon!"

The Cow who Jumped over the Moon

"Well, I'm afraid that is unbelievable, Daisy," said Harry Horse. "No one can jump over the moon. That's just a fairy story."

"Well, I can," said Daisy, stubbornly. "And I can prove it! You can watch me do it if you like!"

The other animals all agreed that they would very much like to see Daisy jump over the moon.

"Meet me here in the field tonight, then," said Daisy to them. "When the moon is full, and the stars are shining bright."

So that night, when the moon had risen high up in the sky, the excited animals gathered together in the field. The rest of the animals from the farm came along too, for word had soon spread that Daisy, the cow, was going to jump over the moon, and they were all eager to watch.

"Come along then, Daisy," said Swift, the sheepdog, as the animals waited impatiently. "Are you going to show us how you can jump over the moon, or not?"

All the animals laughed because they thought that Daisy was just boasting, and that she would not really be able to do it.

"Yes, I am going to show you," said Daisy, "but, first of all, you will have to come with me. This isn't the right spot." Daisy led the animals across the field, to the far side, where a little stream ran along the edge of the field, separating it from the dark woods on the other side. As they crossed the field, they looked up at the great, yellow moon shining down on them. It looked so very far away. However did Daisy think that she could jump so high?

"Now, stand back everyone, and give me some room," said Daisy. The animals did as they were asked, and watched Daisy with anticipation, giggling nervously. Whatever was she going to do?

Daisy trotted back to the middle of the field, turned, then stopped, shuffling backwards and forwards as she took up her starting position.

The Cow who Jumped over the Moon

"Come on, Daisy," cried the animals, impatiently. Daisy took a deep breath, then ran towards the stream at a great speed.

At the last moment, she sprang into the air, and sailed across the stream, landing safely on the other side.

"I did it!" cried Daisy. "Aren't you going to clap, then?" The other animals looked at each other in confusion.

"But you only jumped over the stream!" said Harry Horse, puzzled.

"Come and take a closer look," called Daisy, still on the far side. The animals gathered close to the water's edge. They looked down, and there reflected in the water, shimmered the great full moon! How the animals laughed when they realised Daisy had tricked them.

"See?" said Daisy. "I really can jump over the moon!" And just to prove it, she jumped back to the field again. The animals all clapped and cheered.

"That was a very good trick!" said Swift, the sheepdog.

"Amazing!" said Silly Sheep. "Could someone explain it to me again, please!"

There Was an Old Woman Went Up in a Basket

There was an old woman went up in a basket,
    Seventy times as high as the moon;
What she did there I could not but ask it,
    For in her hand she carried a broom.
"Old woman, old woman, old woman," said I,
    "Whither, oh whither, oh whither so high?"
"To sweep the cobwebs from the sky,
    And I shall be back again, by and by."

There Was an Old Woman Who Lived in a Shoe

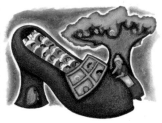

There was an old woman who lived in a shoe,
    She had so many children she didn't know what to do;
She gave them some broth without any bread;
    And kissed them all soundly and put them to bed.

There Was an Old Woman Had Three Sons

There was an old woman had three sons,
    Jerry, and James, and John:
Jerry was hung, James was drowned,
    John was lost and never was found,
And there was an end of the three sons,
    Jerry, and James, and John!

Old Mother Goose

Old Mother Goose, when
    She wanted to wander,
Would ride through the air
    On a very fine gander.

There Was an Old Woman, and What Do You Think?

There was an old woman, and what do you think?
  She lived upon nothing but victuals and drink:
Victuals and drink were the chief of her diet;
  This tiresome old woman could never be quiet.

There Was an Old Woman Called Nothing-at-all

There was an old woman called Nothing-at-all,
  Who rejoiced in a dwelling exceedingly small;
A man stretched his mouth to its utmost extent,
  And down at one gulp house and old woman went.

Mother Hubbard

Old Mother Hubbard
Went to the cupboard
To get her poor dog a bone;
  But when she came there
  The cupboard was bare,
And so the poor dog had none.

She went to the fishmonger's
  To buy him some fish,
And when she came back
  He was licking the dish.

She went to the hatter's
  To buy him a hat,
But when she came back
  He was feeding the cat.

There Was an Old Woman Lived Under a Hill

There was an old woman
  Lived under a hill,
And if she's not gone,
  She lives there still.

Cuddly's Jumper

Cuddly Sheep and Stout Pig were going to show the others how to knit. Cuddly Sheep was really good at knitting. But she needed her friend, Stout Pig, to help with the wool. Stout Pig couldn't knit, not even a little bit, but he was very good at spinning the wool for Cuddly to use.

Wool has to be made into yarn before you can knit with it. Yarn is made by twisting it, like string. That is what Stout did. He collected all the loose bits of wool that caught on thorny bushes around the farm and made long, beautiful lengths of yarn out of them. Then Cuddly used Stout Pig's yarn to knit lots of pretty things. She could knit woolly socks. She could knit woolly hats. She could knit the best woolly jumpers in the world!

Cuddly and Stout sat close to each other. Stout Pig sat with his back against a low hedge and Cuddly sat on the other side. The pig pulled out lengths of wool from a pile under the hedge. He started to spin the wool on his wheel, until it was twisted into yarn. Then he gave the end to Cuddly.

Cuddly made little loops of the wool and put them on two fat knitting needles. Then she started knitting.

"Knit one, purl one, knit two together," she whispered to herself. Only knitters know what these secret words mean. They must be magic words, because they are whispered over and over again.

"Knit one, purl one, knit two together."

The jumper quickly started to take shape. As it grew in size, the animals watching could see it was nearly all white, just like the colour of Cuddly's own woolly coat, with little bits in purple, like the berries on the hedge.

Stout had to work hard on the other side of the hedge to keep up with Cuddly Sheep.

Cuddly looked up. "Is it getting late? I'm getting a bit cold," she said. None of the others felt cold.

"You can put my blanket on," said Pebbles Horse. He pulled his blanket over Cuddly's shoulders. But Cuddly got colder. And colder!

"I keep warm in the straw," said Saffron Cow. She covered Cuddly with straw. But the more Cuddly knitted, the colder she got.

And the hotter Stout became. Cuddly was trying to finish the jumper quickly before she froze. The faster she knitted, the faster Stout Pig had to turn the spinning wheel, and he was soon in a sweat!

Then the jumper was finished… and Cuddly was shivering! Her teeth were chattering! Pebbles looked hard at Stout.

"Where did the wool come from that you were spinning?" he asked.

"I used that bundle of wool under the hedge," said Stout. "It was here when I came."

Pebbles' large head followed the wool from the spinning wheel over the hedge. There was only Cuddly there. "Cuddly," said Pebbles '…I think you have been knitting your own wool!"

Cuddly jumped up in surprise. The blanket and the straw fell off. She was bare all around her middle. No wonder she was cold. Her wool was all gone.

"Oh well," said Cuddly Sheep, taking out the needles from her knitting. "Never mind! I have a nice thick new jumper to keep me warm!"

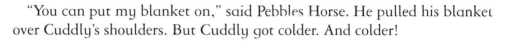

Polly the Potty Postlady

Polly Postlady worked hard delivering letters, and she was always in a hurry. She hated to keep the people on her round waiting – and Mr Price the Postmaster always expected her back at the post office by 12 o'clock.

One morning Polly was in a bigger hurry than ever. She had overslept and was late for work! "Hurry, hurry, rush and hurry!" Polly muttered to herself as she rushed out the door.

"People are waiting for their letters!" Polly Postlady said to herself, as she sped to the post office on her bike. "And Mr Price will be waiting for me!" She zoomed down the street as fast as her bike would go.

"Sorry I'm late, Mr Price," Polly puffed as she flew through the post office door.

"Good morning, Polly!" said Mr Price. "Your postbag is all ready – and it looks very full today!"

"Thanks, Mr Price," said Polly. "I'll really have to hurry, with all those letters and parcels!"

Polly sped down Main Street and tore around the corner of Jackson Road. She was going so fast that she didn't see the removal van in front of her until it was too late! "LOOK OUT!" shouted the removal men. "Oh dear!" shouted Polly, as she flew off her bike. Everything in Polly's postbag went flying, too!

"Oh no! It will take ages to collect all these!" cried Polly, when she had stood up and dusted herself off, "and I'm in such a hurry today!"

The removal men helped Polly collect all the letters, postcards and parcels and put them back in her bag. It wasn't too long before she was ready to go.

But when Polly picked up her bike, she saw that the tyre was flat! "I've got a puncture!" she cried. "I can't ride this now. What will I do?"

"You'll have to walk your round today, Polly," said one of the removal men.

"Oh no!" said Polly. "I'm late enough as it is! I'd better get going!" Polly ran off to deliver the post as quickly as she could.

But she was in such a hurry that she got all the names and addresses mixed up!

Mr Green, on Jackson Road, was expecting a parcel of books. Instead, he got two letters and a gas bill addressed to Mrs Jackson!

Mrs Jackson, who lived on Holly Drive, got a magazine that was supposed to go to Holly Walker!

And Holly Walker, who lived on Green Street, got the parcel of books meant for Mr Green!

Everybody was terribly confused, especially Polly Postlady!

"I must be going potty!" she exclaimed.

Polly rushed and hurried as quickly as she could to try and sort everything out... but by 11 o'clock her postbag was still half full.

She was beginning to feel hopeless, when suddenly she saw something that gave her a brilliant idea.

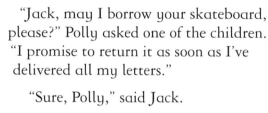

"Jack, may I borrow your skateboard, please?" Polly asked one of the children. "I promise to return it as soon as I've delivered all my letters."

"Sure, Polly," said Jack.

Polly had never been on a skateboard before, but she bravely stepped on. Polly wibbled and wobbled... and teetered and tottered... then she skidded and swayed... and WHOOOOSHED and WHIZZZED down the street.

"Wheeeeeeeee!" cried Polly with glee. "This is just what I need!"

Polly zoomed up and down the street at lightning speed. She had such a good time that the rest of her round seemed to get done very quickly.

"This is much faster than walking," she said, "and much more fun than my bike!"

At last Polly's deliveries were done. She returned the skateboard to Jack, and had just enough time to rush back to the post office.

"I'm back, Mr Price!" she gasped, tripping over her bike as she staggered through the door. "Right on time!"

"I'm glad, Polly," said Mr Price. "And I'm glad you're all right. The removal men brought back your bike. I guess we'll have to mend that puncture right away."

"Oh there's no hurry, Mr Price," said Polly. "I think I've found a much better form of transport for a potty postlady like me!"

Maud
and
the Monster

Maud was a very cheerful but quite mischievous little girl. She also thought she was very brave. All the things which frightened other children were her favourites – slimy eggs, spider's legs, and even the fuzzy bits from Grandpa's razor.

One day, as Maud walked past the cellar door, she noticed that the light was on. Maud thought of all the fun she could have down there exploring and playing games. Without a second thought, she dashed down the stairs. But, as Maud reached the bottom step, she heard the cellar door bang shut – which turned the light off! It was completely dark, and Maud began to feel rather frightened.

Then Maud noticed a strange humming sound. She crept forwards, feeling along the wall, and peered slowly into the darkness. Round the corner she saw a bright, white monstrous shape! Maud screamed!

The cellar door burst open and the light came on. Maud's mum came rushing down the stairs, looking very worried.

"Help, Mum! There's a monster!" cried Maud – but then, as they both looked at where she was pointing, Maud realised it was the freezer!

Maud's mum laughed and Maud felt rather silly. After that she didn't boast about her braveness any more.

When Monsters go to Fancy Dress Parties

We all know what a fancy dress party is. Everyone dresses up as something they are not – a pirate, a king, a princess or a monster. Dressing up as a monster is especially good fun – you can make loud noises and be rude and blame it all on the monster. But what do monsters dress up as when they go to a fancy dress party?

Do they dress up like us? Do they put on their best clothes and think of polite things to say to each other? Do they make sure that they are well mannered, eat delicately and dance modestly?

Oh no! Monsters aren't any good at pretending, they gulp down their food in huge mouthfuls and drop it all over the floor. When they dance they leap about and stamp the floor until it shakes. They hate playing musical chairs because they slip and fall on the messy floor.

So monsters might go to a party dressed like us, but they cannot hide what's inside. They behave in a monstrous way – which I am sure you never do, do you?

Dance, Little Baby

Dance, little baby, dance up high,
   Never mind, baby, mother is by;
Crow and caper, caper and crow;
   There, little baby, there you go;

Up to the ceiling, down to the ground,
   Backwards and forwards, round and round;
Dance, little baby, and mother will sing,
   With the merry coral, ding, ding, ding!

Here's a Ball for Baby

Here's a ball for baby,
   Big and fat and round.

Here is baby's hammer,
   See how it can pound.

Here are baby's soldiers,
   Standing in a row.

Here is baby's music,
   Clapping, clapping so.

Here is baby's trumpet,
   Tootle-tootle-oo!

Here's the way the baby
   Plays at peek-a-boo.

Here's a big umbrella,
   To keep the baby dry.

Here is baby's cradle,
   Rock-a-baby-bye.

How Many Days Has My Baby to Play?

How many days has my baby to play?
   Saturday, Sunday, Monday;
Tuesday, Wednesday, Thursday, Friday,
   Saturday, Sunday, Monday.

Hush-a-bye, Baby

Hush-a-bye, baby, on the tree top,
   When the wind blows the cradle will rock;
When the bough breaks the cradle will fall,
   Down will come baby, cradle and all.

Rock-a-bye, Baby

Rock-a-bye, baby, thy cradle is green;
   Father's a nobleman, Mother's a queen,
And Betty's a lady, and wears a gold ring,
   And Johnny's a drummer, and drums for the King.

Hush-a-bye, Don't You Cry

Hush-a-bye, don't you cry,
Go to sleepy little baby.
   When you wake
   You shall have
All the pretty little horses.
   Blacks and bays,
   Dapples and greys,
Coach and six white horses.
Hush-a-bye, don't you cry,
Go to sleepy little baby.
   When you wake
   You shall have cake
And all the pretty little horses.

Baby, Baby Bunting

Baby, baby bunting,
   Father's gone a-hunting,
To fetch a little rabbit-skin
   To wrap his baby bunting in.

The Baby in the Cradle

The baby in the cradle
   Goes rock-a-rock-a-rock.
The clock on the dresser
   Goes tick-a-tick-a-tock.

The rain on the window
   Goes tap-a-tap-a-tap,
But here comes the sun,
   So we clap-a-clap-a-clap!

Little Kitten

Snuggle up, Kitten,
   warm in your bed.
Let moonlit dreams
   fill your head.

The little bunny
   curled up tight,
Dreams of carrots
   every night.

The baby mouse dreams
   in his nest,
Of cheese, the food
   that he loves best.

Shut your eyes, Kitten,
   sleep and dream,
Of balls of wool,
   and bowls of cream.

Good night!

Mr Moon will guard
   your bed.
"Good night, sleep tight,
   dreamy head."

Index